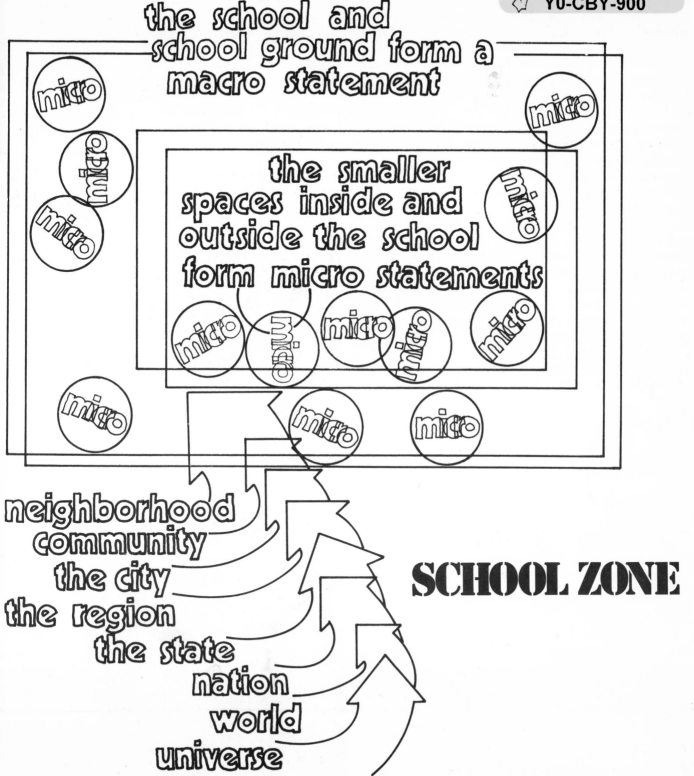

the school and
school ground form a
macro statement

the smaller
spaces inside and
outside the school
form micro statements

micro
micro
micro
micro
micro
micro
micro
micro
micro
micro
micro
micro
micro

neighborhood
community
the city
the region
the state
nation
world
universe

SCHOOL ZONE

SCHOOL ZONE:
Learning Environments for Children
Anne P. Taylor/George Vlastos

our client

 VAN NOSTRAND REINHOLD COMPANY
New York   Cincinnati   Toronto   London   Melbourne

To all children everywhere and to the child in each of us

Page 1

The school should be a microcosm of the larger world, reflecting the unique forces that shape it.

Page 2

(Photo by Dan Aiello)

Printed in United States of America

Designed by Loudan Enterprises

Published in 1975 by Van Nostrand Reinhold Company
A Division of Litton Educational Publishing, Inc.
450 West 33rd Street
New York, NY 10001

Van Nostrand Reinhold Limited
1410 Birchmount Road
Scarborough, Ontario M1P 2E7, Canada

Van Nostrand Reinhold Australia Pty. Ltd.
17 Queen Street
Mitcham, Victoria 3132, Australia

Van Nostrand Reinhold Company Ltd.
Molly Millars Lane
Wokingham, Berkshire, England

16 15 14 13 12 11 10 9 8 7 6 5 4 3 2 1

Library of Congress Cataloging in Publication Data

Taylor, Anne P.
  School zone.

  Bibliography: p.
  1. School environment. 2. Creative thinking (Education) I. Vlastos, George, joint author. II. Title.
LB3257.T35   690.7   74-5950
ISBN 0-442-28454-3
ISBN 0-442-28451-9 pbk.

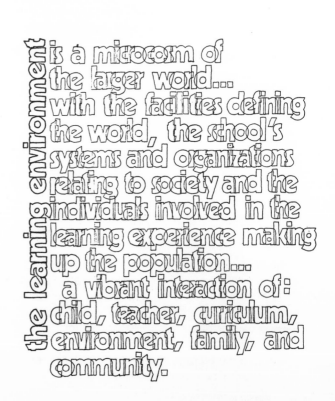

the learning environment is a microcosm of the larger world... with the facilities defining the world, the school's systems and organizations relating to society and the individuals involved in the learning experience making up the population... a vibrant interaction of: child, teacher, curriculum, environment, family, and community.

aknowledgements

The energies of many people have inspired and assisted in the events leading to the publication of this book. We would like to thank the following:

Jack Taylor, Jack Peterson, James Rapp, Richard Britts, and Nelson Haggerson who have helped the authors in their work for many years.

Dan Aiello, Linda Barnes, Ken Carr, Gary Cooper, Paul Halverson, Greg McDonald, Chris Mills, Lyn Pomeroy, Bob Smith, and George Vlastos—a dynamic team who designed an experimental environment for four-year-old children.

Margaret Meyer and Vicki Lund, teachers who brought the prototype environment at Arizona State University alive.

The children and parents involved in the Arizona study.

Palo Alto Educational Systems who helped the authors translate theoretical reseach into practical preschools.

The children and parents of Atrisco and Lowell schools in Albuquerque, New Mexico, and from Santa Clara pueblo.

Rob Strell, our summer shadow. Larry Licht and Jill Elliott for layout help and typing.

Mary Anne Stone's ingenuity in developing the experience directory should be an inspiration to all teachers who value the environment as a teaching tool.

The National Institute of Education, which funded the Southwestern Cooperative Educational Laboratory, making possible some of the research and development on which this book is based.

Michael Braune, a carpenter with an artist's imagination and skill.

Ron Wrona and Adam, our graphic environmentalists.

Barlow Parmenteri—support with a net weight of genius.

Rod Cox and Susan Wooten, landscapists and helpers extraordinaire.

I² staff for their help on perception.

Zomeworks for their research on solar energy and its application to the greenhouse at Monte Vista.

Jimmie Leuder, a principal whose openness to futuristic change should inspire all educators.

To the teachers, parents, volunteers, and children who enthusiastically supported the Monte Vista Project.

Becky Armontrout and Mary Degen.

Donald Kelly, a man with fantastic patience.

Kimberly, Susan, and Meredith Taylor, faithful and understanding helpers.

Don McIntosh, who valued our work and saw its potential.

John Lidstone, an editor with imagination and an eye toward the twenty-first century.

Preliminary editing was executed by Judy Trujillo.

All illustrations, except where otherwise noted, were done by George Vlastos.

CONTENTS

INTRODUCTION

The idea for this book germinated a few years ago, when I was supervising student teachers in schools from the cotton fields of Arizona to the metropolitan area of Phoenix. It was then that I began to notice how the classroom physical settings in which these student teachers were working were all so similar, despite the diversity of locale.

During this time, only a small fraction of the fifty classrooms I visited showed any evidence of children's self-expression. Rather, they were mostly teacher-centered classrooms without areas for independent exploration. And so-called open classrooms were not really open. These classrooms provided little or no way of developing a child's visual literacy, aesthetic appreciation, or motivation for learning. Some classrooms, including those in rural areas near the beautiful Arizona mountains, were without windows. I felt trapped and bored. I wondered how the children must feel.

In the past, educators have tried to improve the quality of education by recommending the purchase of newly designed textbooks and teaching materials, by sending teachers back to summer school, or by holding in-service workshops to "tool up" for better teaching. Sensitivity training and the study of group dynamics has helped teachers in changing the emotional climate of the classroom. But all these changes have not addressed themselves to the crucial issue of the physical learning environment as a support system for education. Despite new training, new textbooks, and greater teacher sensitivity, our classrooms remain approximately the same everywhere—colorless, textureless, and sometimes even windowless.

We have closeted our children for years in sterile monochrome classroom-boxes which house antiquated desks, tables, and inadequate storage systems. There has been little or no relationship between classroom or playground architecture and what is to be taught to children.

How often have children been asked to help design a school? Design criteria given to architects by educators consist mainly of guides for "flexible space." Surprisingly, I found that very little research had been done on how the physical environment affects behavior and learning. Most of what I did find on the topic had been done at prisons and mental institutions, or with rats rather than with children.

The sicknesses of violence, delinquency, depression, destruction, and mental illness have been with us since the beginning of mankind. If the opposite of destruction is creation, we must begin to design an educational system that fosters the creative potential within us all. Perhaps such a creative environment, by bringing out an awareness of the beauty of life, can also bring out the positive values of humanness itself.

In this book, we explore architectural solutions to some educational problems. We consider classroom environments and outdoor play areas as functional art forms—we see them as three-dimensional textbooks. And, we have found through our research, better environments promote better learning through improved reading, writing, concept development, and communication.

At a time when concern for the ecological and the man-made environment is synonymous with survival, excellence in design may help to sensitize people to their surroundings. Therefore, this book offers a process for designing alternatives to present learning environments. We believe that anything can happen, anywhere, and at any time, to help a child learn if the teacher makes full use of an environment which, in turn, is rich enough to excite all the senses of the child and lead him to learning.

Courtesy Educational Facilities Laboratories.

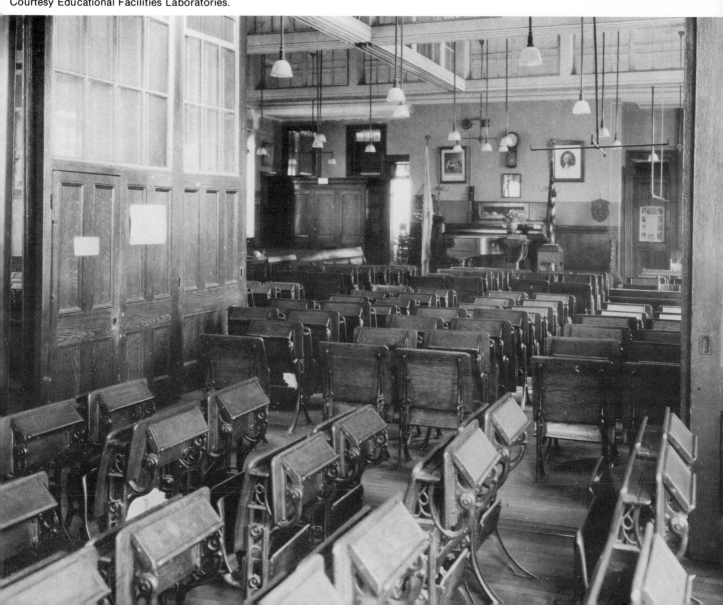

Children's brains are not compartmentalized. They do not learn certain subjects at a specified time of the day. Rather, they are constantly learning, in an integrated way. If a child is an essential part of the learning process, he should be able to make many choices in what he learns, and should be strongly motivated by the excitement which permeates a classroom. He should not be a passive participant, but an active one who can make choices and even change the environment to suit his needs.

This book explores the "how to" of preparing better learning environments, and offers suggestions for parent participation as a way to tap rich community resources and to cut costs in redesigning schools. Old buildings can have a face-lift without exorbitant costs and this remodeling can save the taxpayer's money and eliminate the need for floating large bond issues for new facilities. In short, we want to humanize education.

We want to help children experience the joys of nature and the world around them. This does not mean eliminating technology and its potential for basic education. Although we would like to eliminate some technology, we are not advocating complete overthrow of the present educational system. Rather, we are offering an alternative solution to some very real educational problems along with evidence that the quality of the school's physical environment makes a difference in behavior and learning of children.

We consider all people potential designers. In this book, the term "designer" describes any person without a degree in architecture who influences a space and makes suggestions on how it should be designed and used. Teachers, parents, architects, administrators, and children should be able to use this book as a guide for assessing and improving educational facilities, or for planning new ones. Openness to change is the antidote to the traditional classroom blues.

The term "open classroom" is a state of mind. So-called open classrooms are not really open. Too often, classroom modification does not really affect teaching patterns. Courtesy Educational Facilities Laboratories. (Photo by George Zimbel)

11

1. THE IMPORTANCE OF THE PHYSICAL LEARNING ENVIRONMENT

Some educational historians have suggested that there is more than a casual relationship between the rise of industrialism in the nineteenth century, with its mass production techniques, and the present educational system, which grew up in the same era. The end result is a standardized product, whether it is a car or person, which is formed according to the rigid requirements of a systematized, assembly-line method of production. Consequently, architects have designed schools based not on empirical data or studies of children, but on what society has decided education should be—a hallowed ground in a hallowed hall.

Movement in and out of classrooms is rigidly controlled. Lines are everywhere—to the auditorium, to the cafeteria, to the art room, and to the playground. The pattern of parallel rows in the classroom reinforces these lines. These straight rows tell the student to look ahead and ignore everyone except the teacher. The students are jammed so tightly together that psychological escape, much less physical separation, is impossible. Personal space is often nonexistent or minimal.

Courtesy Educational Facilities Laboratories.

12

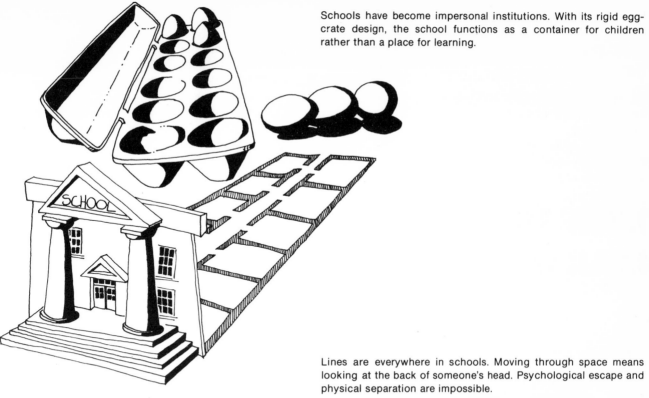

Schools have become impersonal institutions. With its rigid egg-crate design, the school functions as a container for children rather than a place for learning.

Lines are everywhere in schools. Moving through space means looking at the back of someone's head. Psychological escape and physical separation are impossible.

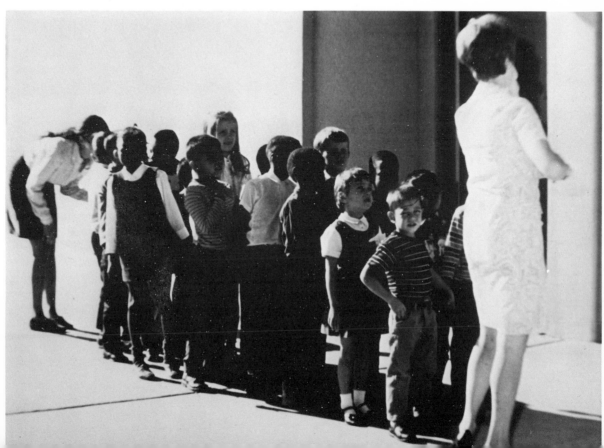

Curriculum as a Design Determinant

With a few exceptions, architects have not studied the child as the user of schools, or assessed his specific educational needs. Architectural plans seldom include suggestions from teachers or children. One premise of this book is that design determinants for school planners should be not only the functional needs of the user, but also the curricular objectives, or what is to be taught. Architecture can teach, and the building itself should reflect what is to be learned. Such objectives can either be strongly intellectual or subtly aesthetic, and should put the child and the teacher in the center of a well-designed humanistic setting.

Thus far, the relationship between curriculum and design has remained relatively unexplored. Educators have been mainly concerned with student behavior, and designers have been busy with budgets and square footage requirements.

In fact, the history of school planning has shown few attempts to combine new educational philosophy, curriculum subject matter, and technology. Pushing out walls and enlarging areas for instructional purposes does not necessarily guarantee a change in teaching patterns. Unless the teacher is trained to perceive the environment as part of the learning process, a traditional pattern of teaching remains, regardless of improvements in classroom size, features, equipment, or design.

Architectural systems can teach; a school design can be three-dimensional textbook. Courtesy Educational Facilities Laboratories. (Photo by George Zimbel)

New Ways to Use Space

The traditional classroom, which limits space and movement and supports the self-contained classroom style, is still with us. Homogeneity of design surfaces and spaces does not stimulate a child's senses. Is it necessary that all school spaces have bulletin boards, chalkboards, a certain kind of chair? Traditional furniture is still used in open classrooms. In many cases, it is unsuitable for open space because, by prohibiting free traffic flow or limiting it to one specific use, the very nature of the furniture belies the term "open."

If education is to address itself to the individual, we need to examine ways to offer an alternative route to that objective. We found a deep desire for personal space among children who were questioned about their classroom preferences. Children seek a place to work and play away from teachers, and sometimes even away from fellow classmates. Schools which simply provide open physical space do not provide for this need. Most playgrounds also fail to provide for this sensitivity. Growing evidence tells us that mere open physical space, especially for children from crowded inner-city dwellings, is not always appropriate. Provision should be made for spaces to hide in and to retreat to as well as spaces for mingling.

Children tell us they need personal space. Learning does not always have to happen in a group. Within open space, architects should provide private space.

Traditionally, educators have felt that students, especially younger ones, should be under surveillance at all times for reasons of moral and physical safety. If children are going to learn the difference between freedom and license, and be responsible for the consequences of their own actions, we need to design spaces in the context of independence and trust. It is the difference between design for democratic living and design for a police state.

A rating scale to assess the physical environment of the classroom gives a designer information and better understanding of the user's needs.

EXAMPLE OF SPACE CHECKLIST

(Only a start in each area, and should be expanded)

Note:
All questions are geared to the child's point of view.

Example of Full Spectrum Analysis

Title:
Children Input within a Given Space

1. Disciplined   1   2   3   4   5   Permissive

Spectrum Subject

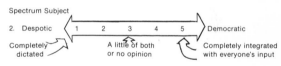

2. Despotic   1   2   3   4   5   Democratic

Completely dictated   A little of both or no opinion   Completely integrated with everyone's input

Note:
The subject is not set up to show that one is better than another—only that a given space leans more toward one attitude than another. Please do not attach a value such as good or bad to the spectrum.

Be consistent in your arrangements of the spectrum so that low numbers (1-3) correspond with the preceding spectrum and the ones that follow. Such as: intense things always to the left and tranquil things to the right.

Scale of a Given Area of Space

1. Large   1   2   3   4   5   Small
2. Overwhelming   1   2   3   4   5   Insufficient
3. Uncomfortable   1   2   3   4   5   Comfortable

Add more

The Need for Variety of Scale and Level

Most schools are adult scaled. Except for some cosmetic modification, such as lowered coat hangers or drinking fountains, we have found that most schools are still designed with the adult in mind. In some of our work we have explored the use of a variety of level changes for sitting, climbing, and crawling. This change of level serves several purposes. First, it breaks down the authoritarian height of the teacher. Unless the adult stoops to the floor, the child rarely gets a chance to look directly into teacher's eyes. The traditional relationship always puts the child in a subservient position; eye to eye contact can promote better communication.

Since learning environments for children must be shared with adult participants, a school needs a variety of diverse scales. This means that some areas can be uncomfortable for an adult, but very comfortable for a young child. The opposite also holds true. The idea of designing a child-scaled utopia is not intended here. Rather, design criteria should be based upon the real world in which the child must negotiate. But, whenever the adult scale interferes with the child's learning flow, the scale should be reconstructed for the child's convenience.

Most schools are adult scaled. Some are still reminiscent of "monumental" styles of architecture.

Some areas should be scaled for children to give them a sense of place.

The Indoor and Outdoor Environment as Part of the Learning Experience

A number of learning opportunities can be woven into the very structure of a school. These may include the way a roof sheds water after a rain, the open display of basic electrical and mechanical functions, perhaps color keyed so children can understand the systems which keep the school operating.

The use of graphics on wall surfaces can enhance learning. Graphics can teach and the possibility of constant visual change increases student interest because it becomes a dynamic rather than a static commodity.

Graphics can also revitalize otherwise barren and sterile surroundings. A perfect example of this happened in a brand-new school in Denver, constructed of concrete block, steel, and glass. When students first moved into the new buildings, vandalism was rampant. Plumbing fixtures were removed, corridor hallways were defaced, windows were broken, and the school grounds were littered with trash. A frustrated art teacher speculated that the school needed some soul—some visual stimuli and some aesthetics. When he and his students designed hall graphics and relief sculptures, the vandalism rate decreased sharply and the students began having greater concern for their environment.

Paint is another way of revitalizing a dull wall surface. Paint can be thought of as a membrane, and it can be changed often because it is an inexpensive commodity.

Mirrored surfaces can teach about space and increase a child's physical and psychological self-awareness. Children who trace their images on a mirror can become more adept at drawing the human figure than those who have no access to their own image.

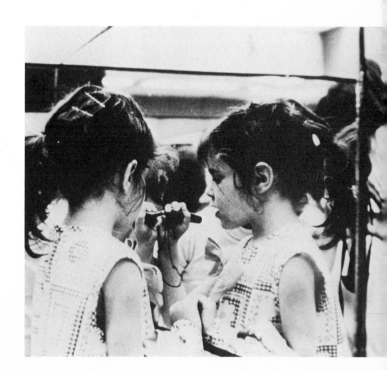

The traditional alphabet pulled by the choochoo train can be replaced by one that divides the letters into straight lines and curves, with color cues for each. Paint can teach and it is a changeable surface. (Design by Ron Wrona)

Surfaces in classrooms can be more than bare walls. A mirrored environment can give children physical and psychological self-awareness.

Versatile furniture design for offices, homes, banks, and factories is very much a part of the contemporary scene. But choices for school furniture are still being made from new catalogs with old ideas and static designs. The design, even of contemporary furniture, is literal and without imagination—a chair is a chair, a table is a table. We are trying to design and offer ideas for more versatile furniture which could serve a multitude of functions.

Storage facilities can contain size and shape discrimination symbols to attract the child and help him correctly classify materials. He could thus be gaining information while he returns supplies and he would also have a place for personal belongings.

Playgrounds have a great deal of potential as learning tools, but they are the least utilized area for this purpose. Trees, grass, earth mounds, flowers, gardens, and greenhouses can teach children about their natural surroundings. Acres of flat dirt, surrounded by chain-link fences, do little to humanize the school. Nor do they help sensitize children to nature and ecological principles so that these become a part of the students' lives. Some schools are experimenting with the idea that the playground can become a municipal park, and thus be used by the whole community.

The area surrounding a school is a very valuable piece of community real estate. How often is it really used by the community?

Chain-link fences give schools the look of a prison. To many children, that is what they are.

The alert teacher can use a well-provisioned environment as a teaching tool. This playground can come alive if you are explaining such notions as *over*, *under*, *around*, *in-between*, and *larger than*, besides providing tangible experiences with nature. We need to start landscaping playgrounds for children. Courtesy Palo Alto Educational System.

Enriched Environments for Cognitive Development

One of the most important sources for the recent emphasis on cognitive learning stimulation in education is the theory of intellectual growth proposed by the child-development theorist Jean Piaget. Piaget has stated that the more new things a child has seen and heard, the more he wants to see and hear. The rate of a child's intellectual growth, then, is a partial function of his environmental opportunity and circumstance.

John Dewey and later progressive educators have stated that experience-centered education is the best way to learn. The British infant school has shown us a way to use experience-centered education in a way that reflects its educational philosophy: Active doing is the best way to learn. In this case, the learning environment must insure quality involvement.

A child needs to use all his senses for learning. It may be more demanding on the adult to provide such learning experiences, but the extra effort can make the difference between existing and living. Courtesy Pacific Oaks College and Children's School.

The more new things a child has seen, heard, and touched, the more he wants to see, hear, and touch. Courtesy Pacific Oaks College and Children's School. (Photo by Gail Ellison Milder)

We talk to children about ecology, but they need experience with it to understand its meaning.

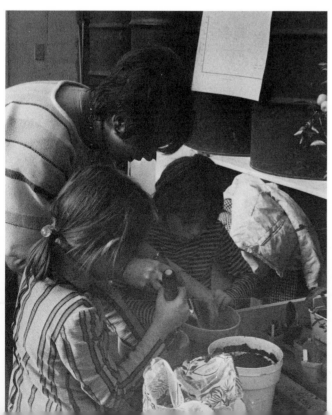

21

Multisensory Learning

Children learn through all their senses. Good teaching should present the child with a variety of multisensory situations in which he himself can manipulate objects, experiment, hypothesize, pose questions, and seek his own answers. Learning, or cognitive growth, occurs only if the young learner is physically and actively involved with his environment.

Maria Montessori has shown that concrete experiences—in prepared environments with specially designed and finely graded materials—provide for optimal learning, from simple to more complex tasks. Environments can be designed so that there are built-in principles of knowledge for young children to discover right in the environment. At orphanages in which tactile stimulation was minimal, children have been found to be far behind in social, emotional, sensorimotor, and intellectual growth as well as in later school achievement. Multisensory learning provides a system that offers many ways to learn. Some children learn better by feeling, and some by seeing. By planning for many ways to gain information, designers are providing for a diversity of learning styles.

Early Learning Center in Stamford, Connecticut. There is more efficient teaching if specially designed and finely graded learning materials are available to children. A richly provisioned environment fosters optimal learning. Courtesy Educational Facilities Laboratories. (Photo by George Zimbel)

Special teaching materials at the Early Learning Center in Stamford. Courtesy Educational Facilities Laboratories. (Photo by George Zimbel)

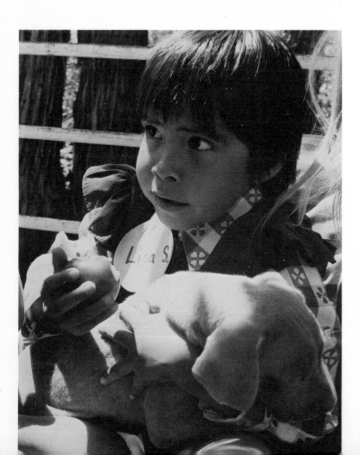

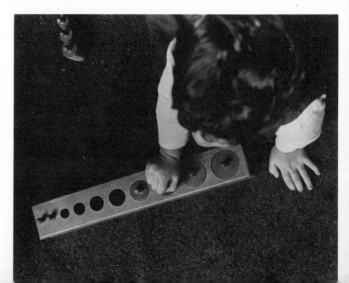

Guided Discovery

Discovery learning is a better teaching method than teacher-centered expository, or the "teacher does all the talking" approach. It is necessary for the architect who designs learning spaces to collaborate closely with the teacher so he can incorporate subject matter into the physical setting.

For example, a simulated archaeological dig for young children might be constructed to help them experience the method of inquiry used by the archaeologist. Sherds, stratigraphic columns, and other items could be buried by older children for the younger scientist to uncover and classify, hypothesize, and generalize. All this can take place in a sandbox. But how many schools have sandboxes?

A water fountain, either inside the classroom or outdoors, can help young children discover, without the aid of an expensive science kit, the properties of water. What sinks? What floats? What is reflection or refraction? Why do stones turn a darker color when they are submerged in water? Is water slippery? Not only is the sound of water pleasing, but it feels good too. Experimenting in this manner can help a child learn a great deal and increase his vocabulary about such knowledge, not to mention the fun and pleasure that water itself can give him.

Technical equipment also can be used for guided discovery learning. Very young children can teach themselves to read by means of a computerized talking typewriter. The feedback to the learner helps him adjust his actions to receive correct information. Such equipment, combined with the use of other well-designed learning tools, as well as natural phenomena, serve to enrich the learning environment and help the teacher make fuller use of it.

Much learning can take place in a sandbox—additive and subtractive sculpture, notions of positive and negative space, or even a simulated archaeological dig.

Early Learning Center in Stamford. Courtesy Educational Facilities Laboratories. (Photo by George Zimbel)

Community Involvement in Education

An educational system can bring parents and community members into the school. We need to ask parents what it is they want their children to learn. If they don't know, educators need to take time to sit down with parents and help them better understand the learning process so they can become an integral part of it.

What a child learns in school needs to be reinforced at home. If it isn't, school learning becomes superficial. If the child's experiences are a starting point for education, then, by definition, his own language and the culture of his home, neighborhood, and community should be utilized in the educational environment. The classroom and outdoor area should play a vital role in reflecting a child's cultural background and his interests. The school can be a microcosm of his larger world. And, if a school is planned to serve community needs, there is no reason for it to be used for only part of the year—it should be used all year.

Change in schools comes from people's energy, not from budgets or square-footage requirements. It is not money which effects change, but the motivation and energy of many people who care and are ready for change.

Some parents have an expertise that no designer can offer. Their energy can help the school reflect the unique architecture of their community. Courtesy Governor Tafoya, Santa Clara Pueblo, New Mexico.

A conservative estimate shows that, in traditional classrooms, the teacher does eighty per cent of the talking. If the teacher feels "on-stage," he limits himself to a narrow level of interaction and communication with the students.

Summary

1. The physical setting of the learning environment does make a difference in, and directly contributes to, a child's behavior and learning. Present indoor and outdoor settings are sterile and inadequate for contemporary educational goals.

2. Children learn through all their senses. Our existing classrooms and teaching methods do not activate all the senses, and thereby cut off some learning potential. Learning environments, and the learning tools with them, must be provisioned for multisensory learning and must be humanized and enriched for more involvement by the child.

3. The curriculum is the design determinant for the architectural concept of the learning environment. A necessary part of designing an optimal learning environment is to initially understand what is to be taught and learned.

4. It is important to understand how the educational setting is to be used. This necessitates intimate communication between the teacher, the children, and the architect.

5. Art and architecture are no longer for the enjoyment of a few. Aesthetics can and should be a part of everyone's daily living. Better aesthetic surroundings help people make better and more critical judgments about the things they buy and their own living environment.

6. The child has a better sense of place if the school is scaled to his size and the setting is humanized. The child can actually help maintain and be responsible for the school with the help of adults. This involvement becomes a commitment and a real contribution to his learning and well-being. To be a functional part of a place where one spends almost the first two decades of one's life would indeed promote a sense of belonging and self-worth.

2. DESIGNING INDOOR LEARNING ENVIRONMENTS

If we were asked to remember a classroom we knew when we were very young children, we would invariably think of the row upon row of slant-top desks and chairs, the expanse of blackboard, and the teacher's desk in its commanding position, overlooking every one of us. There was a place for every child and every child was in his place. These rigid, barren, uninteresting classroom-boxes supported adult authority. For most of us, the teacher, and not the experience of learning, was the center of our early universe.

Although the old classroom did provide a great deal of information, it failed to generate the active and tangible experiences that we know today are a major force in children's learning. This classroom referred the child to the outside world, but did little to make it a part of his everyday learning. The teacher talked of shapes, dimensions, spaces, objects, sounds, colors, and places, but he or she was limited to one-dimensional illustrations on the printed page, the blackboard, or on a sheet of drawing paper.

Tangible experiences are a major part of learning for a child. (Photo by Charles Conley)

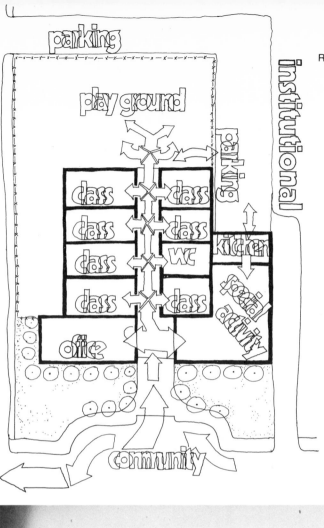

Rigid architectural design reflects rigid education.

All over the country, classrooms look the same—the clock, the alphabet, the blackboard, the flag, the desk. The teacher's desk always seems to be placed in the same spot.

Has the classroom really changed? Perhaps today there are better visual aids and more equipment, and there are chairs that may be placed around circular tables. But essentially children are still learning from pieces of paper. In recent years, parents and educators have come to realize that the classroom must be three-dimensional; it must be an inviting, stimulating environment which in itself can teach the child by encouraging him to use all his faculties and to explore the world he learns in. Instead, as Toffler wrote in *Future Shock*, "our schools fall backward toward a dying system rather than forward to the emerging new society."

Most architects, educators, and school users are aware that our educational systems are not equipped to cope with today's, much less tomorrow's, problems. We must begin to realize now that today's educational systems should be preparing children for an active adult life in the twenty-first century.

In 1847, the Boston Latin School was designed in the shape of a box in support of the "sit and learn" teaching method. Its straight rows of chairs and straight rows of windows were intended to provide ventilation, light, quick departure, ease of view, and a host of needs considered legitimate at that time. Although the United States is changing and educational needs have grown more complex and demanding, classroom-boxes filled with a specified number of chairs in straight rows persist.

Why doesn't the Boston Latin School model meet children's learning needs today?

1. Fixed seating is unsuitable for group discussions and pupil interaction.

2. Rigid seating arrangements do not allow for a variety of activities to take place simultaneously.

3. Sterility and endless uniformity of design in classrooms does not enhance curiosity, but rather suppresses it and reinforces conformity.

4. Classrooms are divided by age groups or subject matter. This concept of learning about one subject at a time, each in isolation from the other disciplines that influence it, is very unrealistic.

5. Monumental architecture reflecting neoclassical styles is inappropriate for the educational philosophies and student needs of today.

6. School buildings are out of scale and proportion to the child participant.

7. Maintenance costs, such as heating and cooling, are a drain on community energy sources but the systems could be revamped to perform more efficiently.

8. The traditional school architecture often reflects a rigid administration, where freedom of movement is restricted and controlled by adults, staff security officers, and bells. Chain-link fences or barbed wire around playgrounds act as barriers to the community and lend a foreboding atmosphere to the school.

9. School designers do not consider the child's specific educational needs or those of the teacher.

What kind of model can we construct for a twenty-first century humanistic approach to environments for learning? The first concept to consider is a definition of a learning environment. The school classroom should be a rich, multisensory environment, with changing stimuli to maximize intellectual development. The design should enhance, reinforce, and stimulate the individual interests and cognitive development of the child. In short, if the child is to become enthusiastic about his schooling, the educational environment should begin to directly relate to children.

A child-centered learning environment is one that uses knowledge of the child as its key source for school design. Relating the school structure to the child user can provide educational gains by making the student more self-reliant and developing a healthy appetite for knowledge. There are many approaches to shaping a learning space that have influenced new classroom design all over the country today. We have made a special attempt in our room designs to consider the child's multisensory approach to learning as well as the teaching curriculum to be used within the learning space.

A tree can be an outdoor classroom. Climbing a tree tells a child about its texture, its form, and how things look from above.

Children seem to like informal grouping.

The Multisensory Child as a Design Determinant

An invitation to an awareness and discovery of the universe awaits every normal child at birth. He discovers the world around him by seeing, touching, tasting, hearing, and smelling. The child is a very keen perceiver. Various tests and observations have shown that he may even be much more sensitive to his surroundings than an adult.

Sensory perceptions are the beginnings of a child's acquisition of knowledge and intellectual development. He has a desire to understand the world around him; he needs to make meaning of things he sees or experiences. Knowledge can be simple, or, as he grows older, more complex and abstract. Information about the world enters the child's brain system through his senses. Bits and pieces of information begin associating themselves, and the child forms concepts. This process of putting bits and pieces together is called synthesis, and leads to knowledge.

How about a playground hammock for resting?

Sight

A child comes from a home where he is undoubtedly exposed to what Marshall McLuhan calls a "hot" medium—television. His sense of sight has been bombarded with action, color, visual humor, and fast, exciting, verbal and nonverbal communication.

To make the sight sense active rather than passive, we need to stand still and really begin to look around us. The alert teacher should lead the child to active seeing by constantly changing the classroom.

Instead of seasonal pictures plucked from outdated files, children's artwork or museum artifacts can enhance the room and interest students. These items should be within the child's scale of vision and not placed at heights where they would become irrelevant to him.

We need to pause and take a real look at the world around us.
Courtesy Pacific Oaks College and Children's School.

If children come from diverse cultural backgrounds, we would encourage teachers to use graphics and materials reflecting those backgrounds. For instance, parents in the Southwest, with their unique multi-cultural heritage and architecture, have complained that classrooms and playgrounds there look no different from those in Wisconsin, Los Angeles, New York, or Chicago. In a predominantly black school, the child might better identify with black artists than with Renoir. The schools on an Indian reservation should strongly reflect where they are instead of using Anglo-made and Anglo-looking materials.

School walls can be painted and the resulting graphics can teach. Children's artwork is the best display item, and the quantity that they produce can provide an ever-changing exhibit. Plants can also humanize an otherwise barren classroom. In other words, the visual environment can subtly use diverse cultural themes and excellence in aesthetics, or it can be very dull, boring and standardized.

Even the most simple graphics communicate. Courtesy Educational Facilities Laboratories. (Photo by George Zimbel)

Paint is an inexpensive way to provide graphics that help stimulate a child's visual perception.

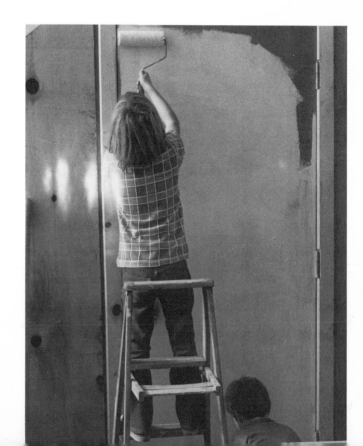

Children who help to maintain a school, feel a part of their environment. Vandalism is decreased when people care.

Sound

Researchers have found that the sound of the teacher's voice permeates the classroom eighty per cent of the time. In our work with bilingual children, we have found that this pattern does not help to foster language development or adequate communication. Children who have difficulty associating alphabet symbols with sound may need to record their own voices by reciting stories, poetry and music, that they themselves compose.

Music is a delight to children of all ages. Shouldn't they have a respectable sound system and listen to good music every day instead of just during the music period? We need to help the child become an acute observer and a more perceptive listener so that he can make intelligent decisions about all the stimuli bombarding his senses.

Touch

Montessori schools help children learn the alphabet by having them trace textured letters with their fingers. Texture is everywhere. Smooth, rough, round, fuzzy, and hard objects can only be discovered by touching. Children also need to be able to describe how things feel.

Unfortunately there is not much to stimulate the sense of touch in present-day classrooms. Surfaces are smooth primarily because they are easy to clean. Unless children go with their teacher on looking and listening walks, they probably have little or no contact with texture in nature.

After reconstructing areas of the classroom with soft fabric, carpeting, and pillows, we noticed that when children entered the area, their behavior immediately changed from active to more subdued. Often they sought a book, begged to be read to, or took a nap.

In our work with very young children, a soft environment helped to develop concepts of soft texture, subdued sound, and pastel color. To a four-year-old child, what is pink? How can it be made from red? We have found that color combined with other sensory cues, such as texture, does affect behavior.

Touching to find out is a part of discovery of the world for all of us. Courtesy Pacific Oaks College and Children's School. (Photo by Gail Ellison Milder)

Early Learning Center in Stamford. Children should have access to good sound systems for listening to music or stories. Courtesy Educational Facilities Laboratories. (Photo by George Zimbel)

34

A round sandbox promotes eye contact and conversation. How does wet sand feel compared to dry sand?

Smell

The sense of smell is important; a child can even sense when his mother is near by her smell. We can offer children olfactory experiences that delineate and identify a particular sense of place. Herbs and flowers grown by children in the playground help them to identify a variety of smells with a particular location. Cooking experiences can help children discriminate among foods not offered in the blander diet of a cafeteria, and also help them to develop a vocabulary to describe smells with better words than "it stinks."

Taste

Closely allied to smell is taste, and perceiving the qualities of bitter, sweet, sharp, sour, or salty marks the difference between oral satisfaction and oral discrimination.

There are many ways for a child to gather information about the world around him, but sometimes we keep him from learning as much as he can by putting him in unstimulating physical settings at school. If we accept the idea that children have sharp perceptions of their surroundings, then we must re-evaluate the kind of spaces we offer them for their education.

Making lemonade and smelling the pungent odor can tell children a lot about the concept "sour". Courtesy Governor Tafoya, Santa Clara Pueblo, New Mexico.

Some sensations intensify with, and even depend upon, close proximity to stimuli, as in the case of tasting or touching. Other sensations may or may not be intensified. The senses of sight, hearing, and smell gather stimuli from very broad areas. When a child moves through a given space, his experience within it will vary although the physical properties of the space remain the same. The child's five senses may thus not necessarily be used to their full potential at all times.

The learning space is defined by both the fixed and the changing elements. The way an individual moves through the space occupied is what varies or changes. The things that remain the same are the participant's five senses, the space in which a learning activity occurs, and the given body of knowledge to be learned. By closely examining the phenomena that remain the same and those that change, the designer can more accurately restructure spaces for more enriching experiences in the learning environment.

There is a distinct difference between hunger satisfaction and taste discrimination. Children need to know the difference.

The child perceives his environment through all his senses. These perceptions help him acquire knowledge and grow intelligently. The richer the environment, the more he will perceive.

The Child's Scale as a Design Determinant

If an elementary school is to be successful in imparting knowledge, and if it is to prepare children for living, it must satisfy the needs of children from the ages of five to twelve years. This age group is a very diverse clientele.

The scale and skill diversity and the specific physical needs of each "generation" within this age group should be important considerations for school architecture. In designing and constructing our environments, we have gone beyond utilization of the floor space alone. An average classroom contains nine hundred square feet. If the room is ten to twelve feet high, we can look at it as containing nine thousand possible cubic feet of space.

The potential uses of this newly found space become exciting to the young child because the space has been planned in terms of his perspective and his scale. Levels and structures, built to accommodate and intrigue a child, do so because they are conceived in terms of what the child recognizes as his surroundings, his height, his reach, his mobility, and his energies. These environments are made for him alone.

Early Learning Center in Stamford. The potential uses of this newly found space become exciting to the young child because the space has been planned for his perspective and size. Courtesy Educational Facilities Laboratories. (Photo by George Zimbel)

In redesigning classrooms we use the total volume of the room. Space utilization becomes more efficient and provides for a number of simultaneous activities.

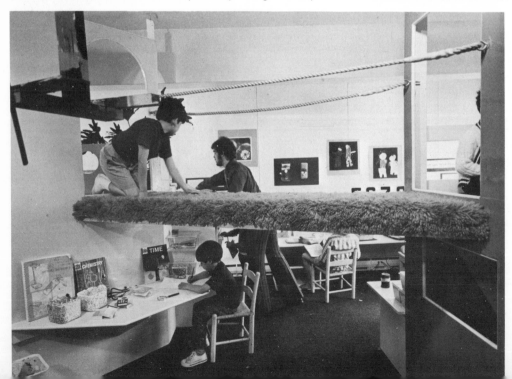

The Child's Skill as a Design Determinant

A child's movement through space and his use of it is completely different from that of an adult. There are many reasons for this phenomenon—children are smaller, more agile, and have a different sense of time than adults. One week is perceived in one way by a second-grader and in another way by an adult. Children devour their surroundings by looking at things from a wide variety of angles, by smelling things up close, by tasting things an adult might never put in his mouth, and sometimes by hearing sounds that pass by most adults as background noise. Children delight openly, and without inhibition, in their experiences.

In studying time-lapse motion pictures of children and teachers in open classrooms (see page 137), we have found differences in the way each utilizes space. The time-lapse process allows us to observe eight hours of activity in three minutes. Because time is concentrated, child and adult movements are intensified, and the difference in movement through space becomes very apparent.

When permitted, the child moves through space rapidly, and darts from place to place. The adult is more stationary when he works with children.

A child's ability to concentrate, even with other activities going on nearby, often amazes adults.

Being able to look at things from a different perspective gives a child a new view of the world. So often they only look up.

Level Changes

Thinking in terms of cubic space or volume is perhaps the most tangible way to begin creative classroom planning. Level changes utilize space that has been empty and nonfunctional for generations.

By dividing up a room with several child-scaled levels, we can give students a sense of place and something they can call their own. Children need places to be and to work, sometimes alone, sometimes with a companion, and sometimes with a larger group. Normal and desirable learning activity requires a spectrum of territorial places.

In an Environmental Preference Interview designed to determine the child's favorite places in the classroom the children drew pictures for us and told us that, in open classrooms, they preferred to be in areas away from the teacher. Details in their drawings showed preferences for the listening center, the art area, the puzzle center, the playground, and others.

The scale of small multilevel personal spaces relate to the child and he to them—they do not overwhelm him. Multiple levels also increase the square footage of a learning area and provide places for several different activities to happen simultaneously, one above the other.

Community Learning Center in Washington, D.C. Well-designed and aesthetically pleasing surroundings have a definite effect on a child's attitude toward school. (Courtesy Educational Facilities Laboratories. (Photo by George Zimbel)

Often the child is confronted by physical factors which make even entering the school difficult. Windows may be placed for adult use at a level where small children cannot easily view the world and learn from it. An adult planner must remind himself that his client's eyeball is at the level of the planner's navel. This means that a school may appear to be twice its size to a child.

Again, unless the adult stoops to the floor, the child rarely gets a chance to look into the teacher's eyes, and then it is usually in a "one down," subservient position. With a variety of level changes, authoritarian perspective diminishes and new interaction patterns are possible.

Level changes facilitate eye-to-eye contact.

St. Louis Priory School Library. Courtesy Educational Facilities Laboratories.

Curriculum as a Design Determinant—
What Should It Be?

One of the most important processes in designing any educational setting, whether it is a room, a school, or a playground, is to use and critically examine information from teachers on what is to be taught by them and learned by the child. Educational history has shown that ideas about curriculum have changed over the years, almost in pendulum fashion. Therefore, there are diverse ideas about what curriculum should be.

Assessing the Curriculum

We have found in our many conversations with both parents and teachers that they are sometimes unable to verbalize learning priorities for their children. When we sit down with teachers to explore their curriculum, we set aside many hours because it takes time. Teachers need to tell us what the basic concepts are at a given developmental level in such fields as math, science, language arts, music, and art, and in the child's personal, social, and physical growth. This time is well spent. It is a fruitful and rewarding experience and gives the designer much more information than if he were working in isolation at a drafting board with little more knowledge of the user than the fact that he needs "flexible space."

Most of our experience in this process of eliciting curriculum information has been with teachers of young children, but the approach is applicable to other ages as well. In this era of rapid change and knowledge explosion, it is necessary to find alternative ways to teach the content of each discipline. We must give the child an optimal environment to help him discover and learn about an ever-increasing body of knowledge.

Curriculum has traditionally been divided into subject matter areas with portions of time allotted to the study of each subject. We could once assume without question that the phrase "to teach the sciences" meant to teach their content, or the body of the scientists' conclusions. But even as early as the second decade of this century, the growth of knowledge forced us to modify this view. It has become a question of determining just what knowledge is of most worth to the clients of the schools. This is why we have asked teachers to work with us and define their curricular objectives. It is a streamlining process. It builds a system for organizing the universe so that the child can begin to discover some order within it through a rich and well-developed compilation of media and materials, instead of a haphazard collection of leftovers from previous years.

A bird's-eye view of an experience-centered classroom in a traditional setting vividly illustrates the many activities which can take place simultaneously.

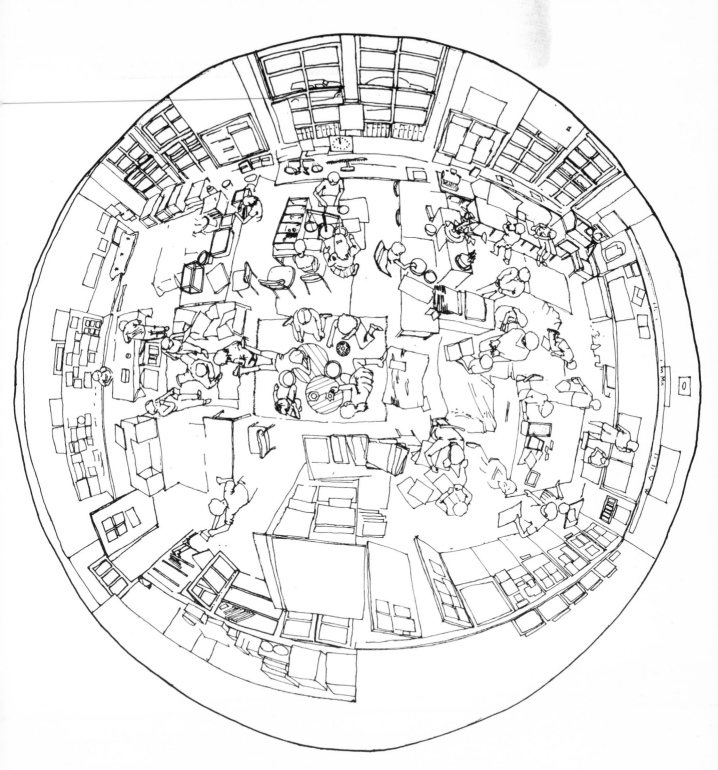

Interdisciplinary Concepts as Design Cues

Concepts help the child make sense out of his world, as he labels, classifies, and groups similar objects and ideas. The architectural learning environment can be designed around a core of such concepts to complement and support the curriculum and the smaller instructional manipulatives within it. The nature and level of the child's perceptual awareness should dictate the mode and manner of involvement with the media and materials used. The child learns in a multisensory way as he interacts with people, places, things, and ideas and the stimulus for learning comes from a combination of the curriculum to be learned, teacher prescription, child interest, and happy discoveries.

The learning materials might include organic objects, artifacts, children's literature, movies, films, filmstrips, slides, tapes, lighting, music, found objects, art reproductions, sculpture, toys, animals, and artists' materials—or any other object which reinforces the learning of a concept. Well-organized environmental stimuli help the child to gather and store information more efficiently. They offer the possibility of diversified thinking about one concept, rather than a compartmentalized process where the concept must be thought of separately in math, science, or art. In our system, the concept is learned in an integrated way and is seen in all its possibilities and from many angles. A feedback loop of questioning tells the teacher just how much about the concept has been learned.

For example, a knowledge of machines is a part of every physical science curriculum. No matter how complex they are, all are based in some way on six simple machines—the lever, the fulcrum, the wheel axle, the pulley, the inclined plane, the wedge, and the screw. Concrete examples of these simple machines can be designed into the physical environment of the school to give children experience with machines as an integral part of the architecture. Other related materials could then reinforce the machine concepts.

The six basic machines, part of the science curriculum, can easily be incorporated into the architectural systems of a school.

SIX BASIC MACHINES

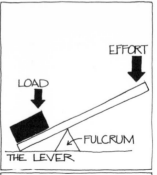

THE LEVER

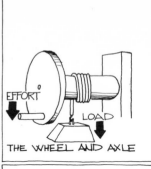

THE WHEEL AND AXLE

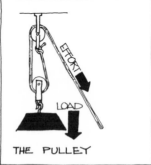

THE PULLEY

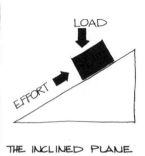

THE INCLINED PLANE

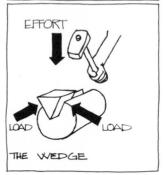

THE WEDGE

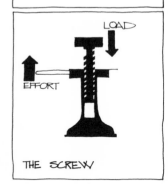

THE SCREW

The space frame table, a new concept in classroom furniture, is a good illustration of one of the six basic machines. The pulley system raises the table to the ceiling, providing truly open space when the table is not needed, as well as more functional use of ceiling space.

SPACE FRAME TABLE

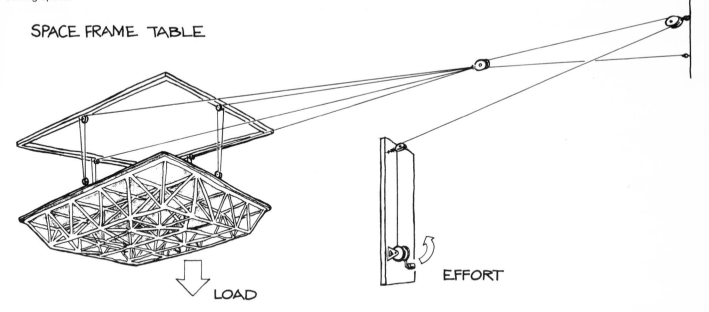

LOAD

EFFORT

Identification of representative ideas from all the disciplines is one way of solving the problem of the great increase in knowledge. Once this is done, it is possible to assess where ideas are shared by a number of disciplines. In this way, a system begins to develop for organizing teaching materials around a specific concept. This assists the teacher and designer in integrating these meaningful materials into an optimal learning environment. Furthermore, these materials can be so organized that they move from simple to complex, so that every child interacting with them can develop his own concepts at his own developmental level.

No two children experience the primary data of an environment in the same way. Thus, once built, an interdisciplinary organizing system is useful not only for the classroom architect, but for the teacher as well. In summary, the process involves the following:

1. Definition of the main concept to be learned from each discipline at a given developmental level.

2. Making an interdisciplinary system to see where concepts overlap.

3. The teacher's knowledge of her sources so she can best equip the environment to teach concepts, preferably based on child interest.

4. The teacher being free from traditional textbooks to use the environment in the most creative way possible.

5. The teacher having the ability to question, reinforce, and bring the environment alive to the child at any time and at any given place.

6. The outcome should be an enriched, ever-changing, stimulating, and systematically organized environment so that the teacher can seize on a child's interest to help him understand and become sensitive to his universe.

7. The child's acquired sensitivity not only includes his accumulation of knowledge, but also how he uses it to live, and how he expresses himself creatively in music, song, dance, art, or play.

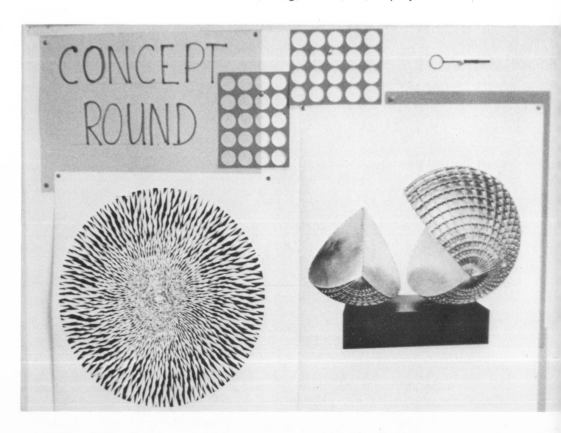

A well-chosen, thematically organized system of curricular materials gives children concrete examples of the concepts that they must know. Teaching materials should be chosen wisely.

3. GUIDE TO PLANNING A LEARNING ENVIRONMENT IN AN OPEN CLASSROOM SETTING

Planners of learning spaces should consider some of the following criteria before going ahead with detailed plans. It may not always be possible to adhere to these criteria, especially in cases where teachers are not even hired until after the new school is designed and built. The ideal situation would be to formulate designs by consulting all the staff members who will be using the space. The following plan is based on an experimental renovation project at the Monte Vista School in Albuquerque, New Mexico.

Life Safety Code

When one is advocating learning alternatives and new methods of space utilization, it is important to understand the responsibility of the designer to the well-being of all users of a creative learning environment. The Life Safety Code is the safety standard governing all schools in the United States. The code should be thoroughly understood before one embarks upon a rearrangement of space. The code should not be viewed as a deterrent to creative design, but as a guide to proven safety conditions. If there is a conflict between design details and the safety code, each community can present its case to local officials for a clarification. Often, the code does not coincide with a philosophy of open education, but, on the whole, the code is a good yardstick for school design.

The Study of How the Space is Used

1. Make a simple floor plan of the room to be built or redesigned.

2. Assuming you are examining an open classroom, identify each area of the room, and have teachers show you specific instructional areas of interest centers, and how each one will be used.

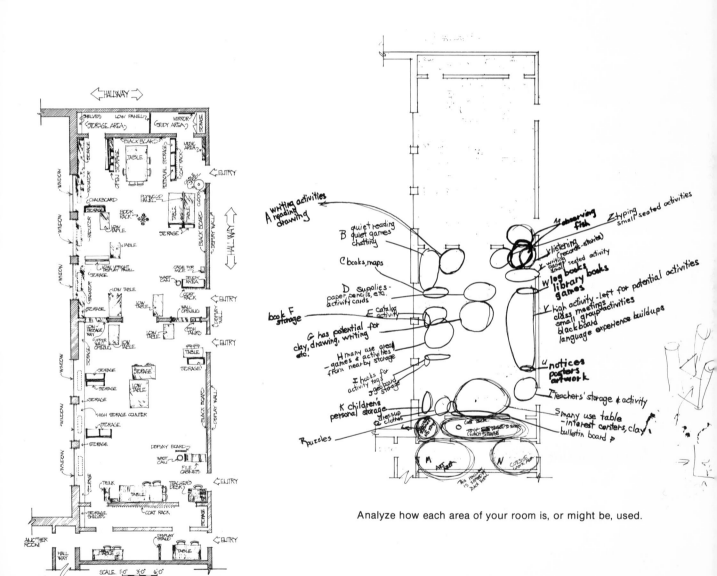

Analyze how each area of your room is, or might be, used.

To examine how your classroom is used, make a simple floor plan. Get the children to help identify where activities take place. Have them draw a plan too.

3. Analyze the circulation of traffic among the instructional areas. How often is or will an area be used? With teachers? With children alone? All the time? Part of the time?

4. What teaching techniques will be used within the learning space? Small group instruction? Independent learning? Discovery learning?

5. Indicate whether or not the activities within the interest centers will be predominantly active or passive.

6. Study each center in relationship to the others. What do they have in common? What are their differences? What activities could be combined? Which centers could be located close together? Which concepts to be taught will be integrated from several disciplines?

7. Think in terms of combining centers that have overlapping concepts and potential experiences. The math and science areas in the Monte Vista project were combined into one.

8. Decide which centers could be located on the ground plane and which could be housed on an upper level.

9. Decide where to place smaller interest areas in the context of the total room volume. A small interest area means just that—there should be just enough space for a limited number of students; this area is not designed for use by the whole class.

10. Define what you need in terms of storage for each area. Proper and orderly storage of the learning tools is a necessity for efficient learning.

11. Ask the teachers if the children are responsible for paper storage, art material storage, or other housekeeping.

12. Coordinate concepts and curriculum goals with storage design. Messy and cluttered facilities are distracting elements in classrooms where children are trying to develop perceptual skills for reading.

Proper and orderly storage of learning tools is a necessity for efficient learning.

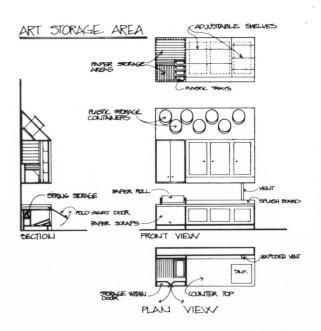

An art storage area makes order out of chaos.

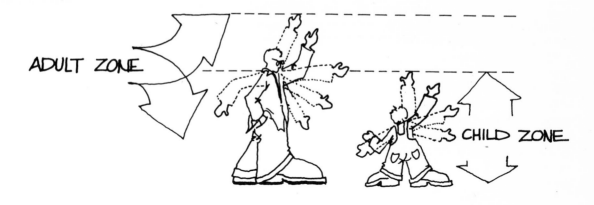

ADULT ZONE

CHILD ZONE

Child access to storage promotes independence, and makes children feel responsible for their environment.

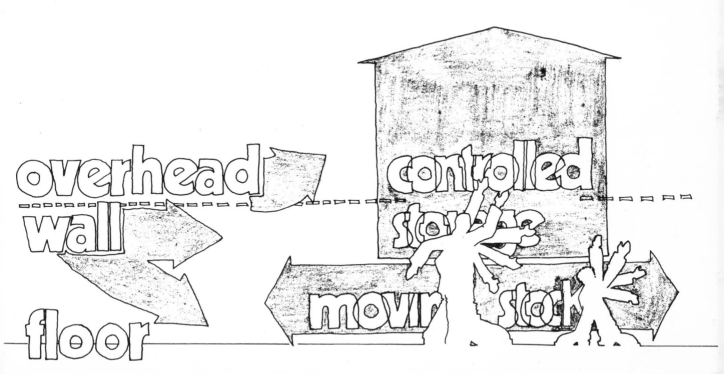

overhead
wall
floor

controlled
storage

movir stck

Child storage consists of moving materials. Adult storage is more controlled and static.

Large Multiuse Area Within the Classroom

There should be an area with ample space for the whole class to gather easily and work together comfortably. The following are points to be considered in its design.

1. This area should be completely free of obstacles so that it can accommodate active student movement.

2. The area should be flexible and manageable so that it can be quickly converted to many uses.

3. There should be enough space for the peripheral experience centers to spill into the open area at any given time.

4. The open space should be a neutral area to facilitate synthesis learning from two or three experience centers.

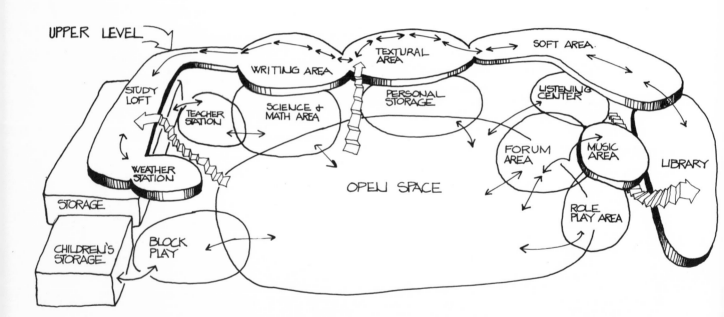

A large central open space could be used for a synthesis of some of the surrounding activities and experiences. Note upper levels that overlook the open space.

Traffic Flow

The study of traffic flow into, out of, and around the classroom is an important design criterion in order to achieve efficient and functional circulation of students and teachers.

Traffic patterns should be convenient and facilitate, not interfere with, the educational function of the classroom.

A variety of paths from one part of the learning space to another should promote easy coming and going between exits, individual learning areas, second levels, and storage areas.

Traffic flow should also reflect scale and the different body agility of a child and an adult. Scaled-down traffic routes motivate a child to take interest in areas he might not otherwise visit. But this may also mean that an adult has to stoop or crawl on hands and knees in certain areas. Certainly this kind of room is no place for a timid adult.

The Monte Vista project children's entry opens into a child-scaled, child-maintained coat room, and leads to a personal storage area. The entry is functional for children because it leads to "their" area. To simply install a child-sized door leading to an area without a specific purpose, does not insure the door's use.

Regulations call for open-ended access, especially on second-level ramps. General alternatives should be considered in designing a variety of access routes.

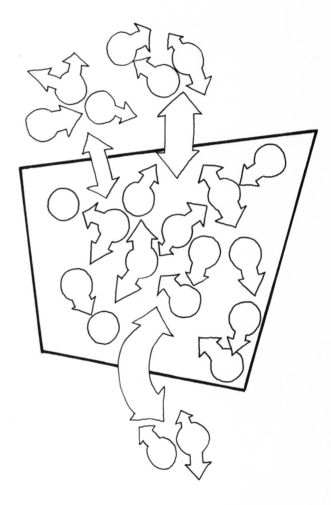

Fluid traffic patterns in a classroom provide a means for better communication.

Storage as a Learning Experience

Classroom housekeeping has always been a problem, but it is especially cumbersome in the experience-centered classroom where it is necessary to have many manipulative materials for "hands on" learning. Where do things go? Stacks of cardboard cartons cluttering a corner of the room do not facilitate good learning habits.

Even though the child does not seem to be disturbed by what adults would consider chaos, putting things away and making the room ready for the next day helps him be responsible for the orderliness of the room. In this way, the child can appreciate that pencils are sharpened and ready for work, and that someone else hasn't stepped on or lost a piece of a favorite puzzle. In our affluent society, we have not taught enough respect for preserving things. It always seems that if something gets broken, children are placated by a sympathetic adult who says, "don't worry, we'll get you another." Perhaps the days of unlimited consumption are rapidly coming to an end.

Who has access to the learning materials? Some

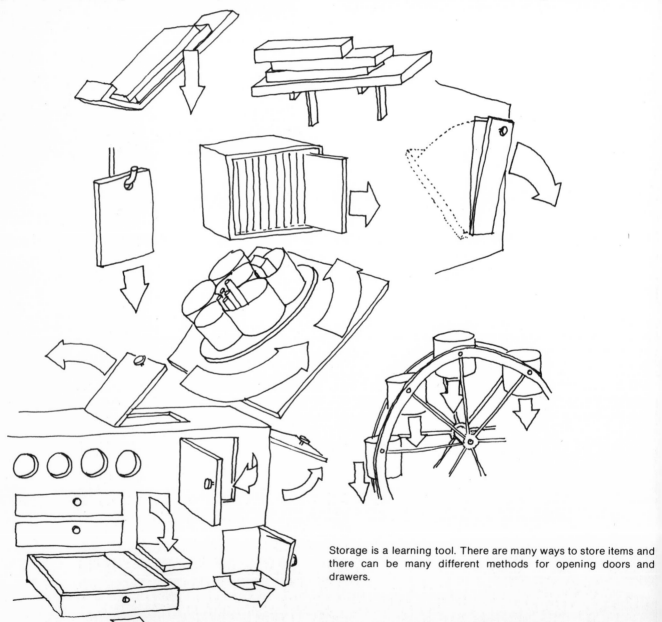

Storage is a learning tool. There are many ways to store items and there can be many different methods for opening doors and drawers.

54

children, or all? Are children responsible for putting away their materials? In considering storage design, we must look out at the total volume of the room.

Children and instructors alike can set up cycles of interaction with the materials stored in the learning environment. These circulation patterns should be determined by the location of the stored articles and the areas in which articles are to be used, as well as the time involved in taking and using the article, and returning it to its storage area.

To tote a fishing tackle box filled with his own pencils, crayons, and rulers to the working area he chooses, delights the child. When space is shared with a number of other children, many a child wishes he could take an "Alice in Wonderland" pill and jump into his own highly personalized space.

A bank of storage boxes serves as personal storage space for fifty-five children.

Activities Facilitated by Storage

Storage can be arranged to complement the activity next to it, or it can change the activity performed in a given area by the nature of material which is stored adjacent to that area.

Since stored material influences to some degree the type of learning activity which takes place adjacent to it, storage areas can bring flexibility to the learning environment. With movable storage areas, the function of the room can be reorganized and thus allow for new experiences within the classroom. Students as well as teacher can experiment with the environment by occasionally changing around the storage areas.

The ability to change the environment gives children a concrete example of how the form of a room should follow its function. This experience also gives the students a chance to make choices and decisions and to see the environment change rather than remain static.

It is possible to design a variety of manipulative functions with storage activity. Various physical properties—for example, the force of gravity—can be emphasized by well-designed storage areas that include a juxtaposition of storage planes.

Storage can be arranged to complement the activity that takes place nearby.

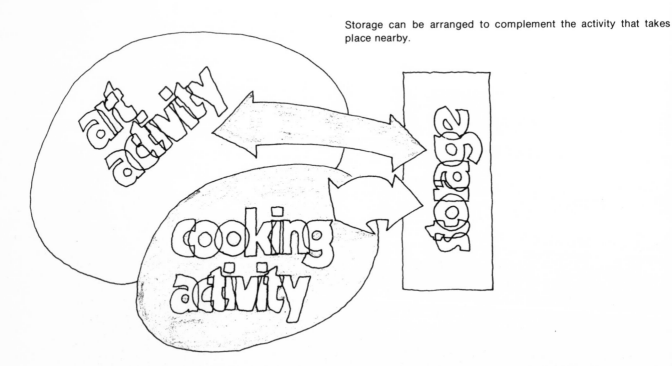

An environment with flexible storage systems that are related to activities gives children a concrete example of how form follows function.

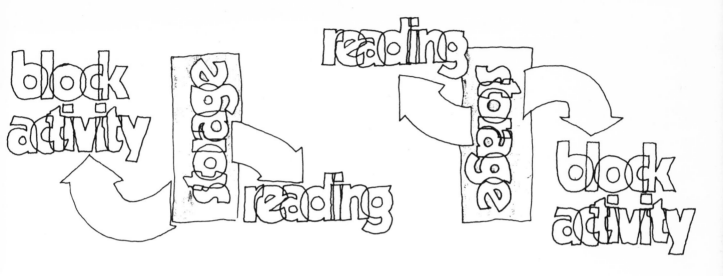

Movable storage systems provide flexibility of space usage.

Furniture in the Classroom

Research has told us that furniture and its placement greatly influences group behavior. In educational settings, the most interested students sit where there is maximum visual contact with the instructor. A teacher can tell a lot about herself by where her students sit. She can tell even more if the pupils have freedom of movement and of choice. In traditional classrooms where rows of desks dominate the floor plane, there is little choice and very little communication among students, except with the back of someone's head.

As mentioned in the first chapter, furniture designers to date have limited their creative energy to contemporary commercial and home furniture. But school furniture has been sadly neglected. We have found that with very young children, well-designed furniture can have a variety of functions—it can be used for more than one activity, it can reinforce curricular goals, and it can even promote better social contacts and communication.

We also have found that the use of well-designed free-form objects stimulates a child's creative play and that he can make the furniture become whatever he wants it to become. Literal toys and furniture produce literal play.

In this type of furniture arrangement, very little communication can take place.

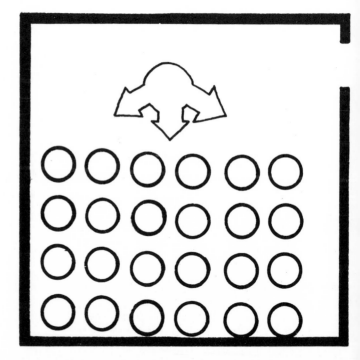

Where teachers do most of the talking, learning is limited to listening and other sensory learning is cut off. This is an antiquated system of teaching and has no place in a democracy.

We need newly designed furniture that will not become obsolete and that will serve a multitude of functions.

School planning and furniture design are not exempt from obsolescence. These discarded desks are still available in school furniture catalogs.

Early Learning Center in Stamford. Models of good design can help children make better aesthetic judgments about their own surroundings. Courtesy Educational Facilities Laboratories. (Photo by George Zimbel)

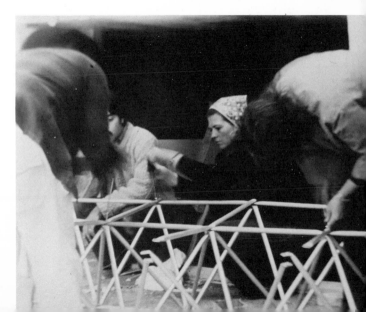

Alternative Solutions for Design

You don't necessarily need a large budget to change the inside of a classroom or to invent alternative furniture. Here are a number of ideas for limited budgets.

Plastic or large slabs of wood are functional as tables and are often better if they rest on blocks or bricks. When not in use, they can be stacked and stored so that the space they take up can be used for other activities. In fact, untraditional furniture can often be used for whimsical functions to the delight of young children.

Pillow possibilities are endless. They can be made by children, parents, or older students and they can be constructed in a variety of colors, textures, and shapes.

Fabrics can add color to any room and are an inexpensive way to change the color quality of any space. Bold patterns on well-designed fabrics catch a child's attention and develop his aesthetic sense. Batik or tie-dyed fabrics that the children have printed themselves are excellent ways to divide space in a classroom. Stretch fabric also has interesting uses—it can be pulled and fastened into forms and curves based on mathematical concepts to give a child some knowledge of architectural principles.

Sign and billboard companies sometimes give away unused billboards, which can be adhered to any surface with wallpaper or wheat paste. They offer a simple and quick solution to the problem of color modulation.

Lighting is a tricky design problem, even for homes. To see well for reading is not necessarily the proper criterion for a listening area, or for a quiet resting area. Alternative, and often less expensive, lighting systems can humanize a setting; rows of fluorescent fixtures will not. Lighting can even be a means of changing color in the classroom—or perhaps for changing moods.

Space frame table installed in an open classroom. Note the soft forum area for large group instruction.

Blocks with a top of plastic or wood can be used as a table. When not in use, the parts can be stored or used as play structures. Movement and flexibility are essential in designing furniture for open classrooms where space is needed for a variety of experiences.

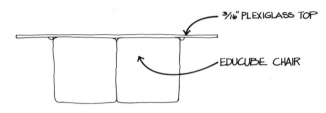

3/16" PLEXIGLASS TOP

EDUCUBE CHAIR

EDUCUBE TABLE
©

Soft pillows in a hard building can change the mood and feeling of the classroom. They also change the behavior of the children.

To a four-year-old child, what is positive and negative roundness, spherical roundness, or cylindrical roundness? Even pillows can provide learning cues.

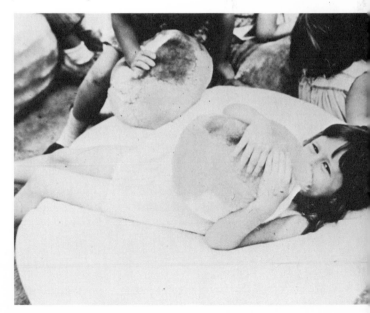

Solutions to Design Problems Using Curriculum as a Design Determinant

Soft Environment

Concepts and skills to be learned	Design suggestions for teaching the concepts
Concept of soft textures.	Soft fabrics as space definers.
Subdued sound—sound can be absorbed by fabric.	Soft textures as the delineation elements of the space—carpets on the floor, low, soft ceiling plane, and soft textures surrounding any rigid structural elements within the space.
Pastel color.	Overall use of pastel colors.
Emotional aspects of a soft environment: Either passive play activities such as role play and story telling, or soft aggression activity such as pillow fights and pouncing activities.	Design structure to receive children sitting quietly and resting, or involved in pulling, pushing, and pouncing activities.
Psychomotor skill development.	Structure should be manipulated by children and redesigned at a moment's notice.

A soft environment can be an inviting place to relax. It can offer the experience of soft texture, subdued sound, and pastel color. (Photo by Charles Conley)

Geometric Environment
Concepts and skills to be learned

Two- and three-dimensional geometric concepts.

Primary color.

Experiences with uncommon perspectives of space.

Large muscle development.

Discovery of geometry by wandering and playing within a geometrically inspired space.

Design suggestions for teaching the concepts

Integrating different geometric shapes, both positive and negative, within a given space.

Primary colors for articulating both two- and three-dimensional geometric shapes and forms throughout the environment. Use of color to define form.

Organizing the shapes so that level changes can act as traffic paths to lead children through, up, over, and under a three-dimensional collage of forms and shapes.

Large shapes built for large muscle play and exploration.

Use of spaces created by geometric shapes to facilitate small group learning as well as role playing possibilities.

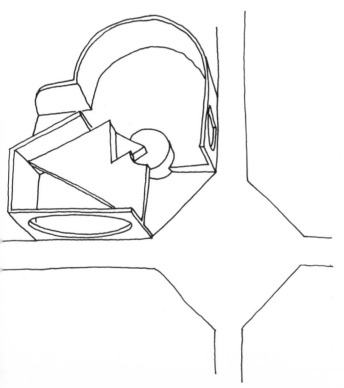

A geometric environment gives children mathematical cues related to the recognition of forms. This skill is a foundation for reading.

Color reinforces geometric shapes. It is a vital part of math, art, perception, and reading readiness. (Photo by Charles Conley)

Organic Environment
Concepts and skills to be learned

Design suggestions for teaching the concepts

Science, math, and art concepts with organic materials—what floats, what sinks; reflection and refraction of wet objects.

Water fountain; wet and dry sand tables.

Motor skill development

Balancing circle, rope maze, and sloping surfaces.

Socialization, communication, and vocabulary development through peer interaction, and visual contact.

Circular working areas and comfortable surfaces to stimulate socialization. Round areas promote better communication than rectangles.

Spaces for comfortable adult and child interaction.

Level changes for eye-to-eye contact between teacher and student.

A system of architectural units based on curricular objectives becomes a three-dimensional textbook for the young child.

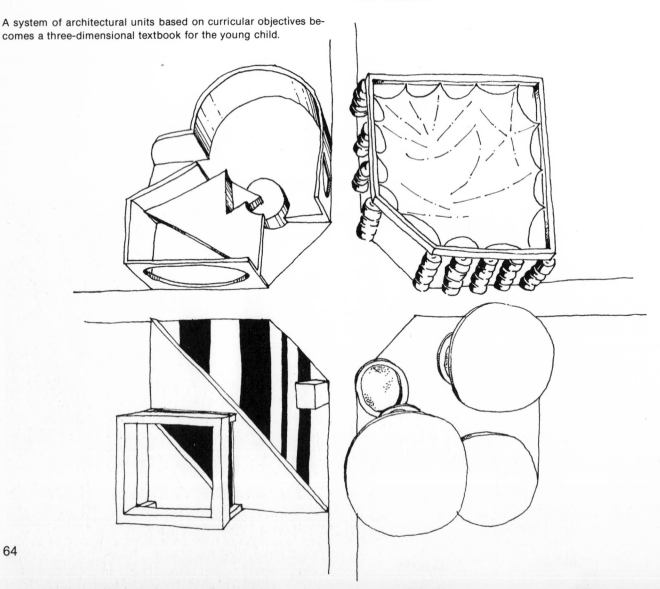

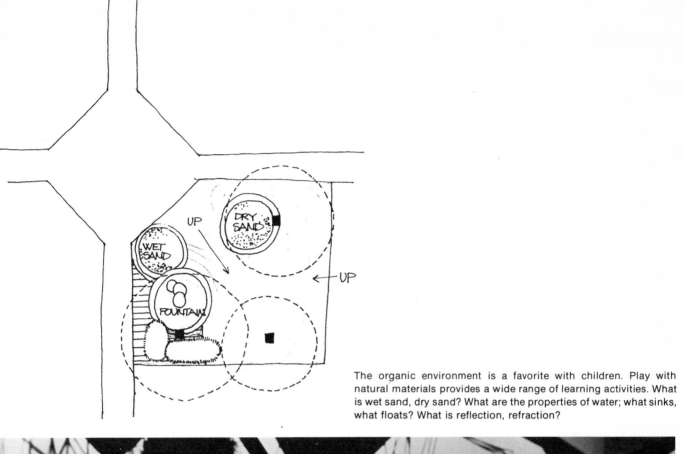

The organic environment is a favorite with children. Play with natural materials provides a wide range of learning activities. What is wet sand, dry sand? What are the properties of water; what sinks, what floats? What is reflection, refraction?

Entry

Concepts and skills to be learned	Design suggestions for teaching the concepts
Concept of a child's own scale.	Small entry geared to a child's proportions rather than those of an adult.
Concepts of measurement and comparison (smaller, larger).	Child-scaled entry.
Body anatomy	Positive and negative space in the shape of a child's body for the design of an entry brings awareness of body parts.
A child's sense of place.	A marked distinction, discernible by the child, between doors to be used by him and those to be used by adults.

Teacher Station

Concepts of teacher needs	Design suggestions for teaching the concepts
Personal space that is also adjacent to the learning activity in the room.	Locate teacher area away from the mainstream of classroom activity and traffic.
Planning center for teachers and parent-teacher meetings.	Create an atmosphere that will encourage the teacher to use this space as his or her own planning center.
Limiting children's access to the space without using doors or other barriers. (They can learn to respect adult personal space if they know the adult respects theirs.)	Design this area specifically for an adult so that large proportions of chairs and desks, or different carpeting, will subtly discourage young children from spending a great deal of time in the teacher station.
Storage for items used infrequently by the children.	Locate a generous amount of storage next to the teacher area for materials used only occasionally in the learning space.

Mirror Environment

Concepts and skills to be learned	Design suggestions for teaching the concepts
Active and passive activity through the use of mirrors and kaleidoscopic phenomena. This should include reflection, refraction, infinite space, and optical illusions.	Strong, heavy-duty mirrors that can be cleaned easily and that can withstand a lot of drawing and writing activity.
Self-concept activities.	Mirrors arranged so that a child can study himself in a variety of angles.
Role-playing and theatrical makeup activity.	A mirrored area large enough to allow for a group of four or five children.
Cultural awareness.	Area should be located where children can try on museum-supplied clothes that reflect different cultures.
Adult participation, from outside the mirrored area, to facilitate activity and language development.	Area should utilize the child's scale for access, allowing the adult to stand nearby.

Mirrors are essential to self-awareness. Children who trace their image on a mirror produce more detailed drawings of the human figure. (Photo by Larry Licht)

Mirrors can enhance physiological and psychological awareness. Theatrical makeup gives the child a better sense of his own face.

Forum Area

Concepts of function needs	Design suggestions for concepts
A comfortable area that is convenient for large and small group meetings. It should accommodate passive as well as active activities.	Forum should seat all the participants in the room at once. It should have soft cushions arranged on many different levels so all can see. Cushion covers should be easy to clean. Colors should act as a unifying element for the whole room.
Music area for instrument storage, and room for three to five children to explore their musical interest.	Music area should have enough storage for instruments as well as room for playing them. This area could be elevated and integrated with the soft forum if a large group wishes to work on musical instruments or act as an orchestra for a performance.
Listening area with a tape recorder, a record player, an AM-FM receiver, and an area with earphones where children can listen to audio material. This activity area should also have movie and slide projectors.	Listening area should have storage for all electrical equipment so that the teacher has control of making it available according to convenience and study plan. This would require locks and various cabinets for secure storage of expensive equipment. Arrange storage so that it does not interfere with the activity in the listening-area space. The various surfaces should be used for sitting, standing, equipment, installation, and storage.
Role-playing area with activities related to a stage and forum area.	Role-playing area should accommodate specialized storage such as clothes and creative costumes, makeup, puppets, and dramatic props. Integrate this area with the soft forum and the stage in the front of the forum.

The soft forum, with cushions arranged on different levels, as in a theater, is a comfortable area for group meetings.

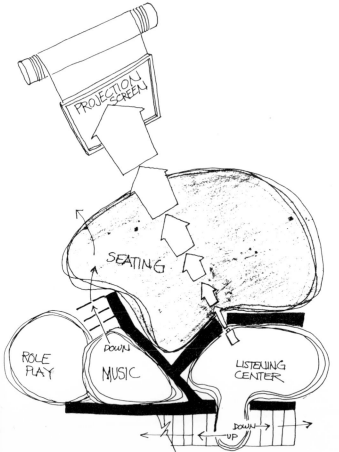

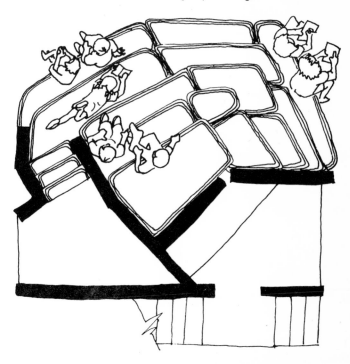

A gathering place can be used for meetings and for instruction. The surrounding areas, designed for specific activities, add to its use.

Open Space Area
Concept of function needs

A flexible open area.

An area for synthesis to take place from any combination of interest areas.

Open physical space to act as a visual relief and as a natural focus for large activities.

Design suggestions for concepts

An area with very few structural barriers or supports.

A large open area with its perimeters defined by many areas of activities.

Furniture should complement the versatility of the space. Requires furniture that could be quickly stored and rearranged with as little effort as possible.

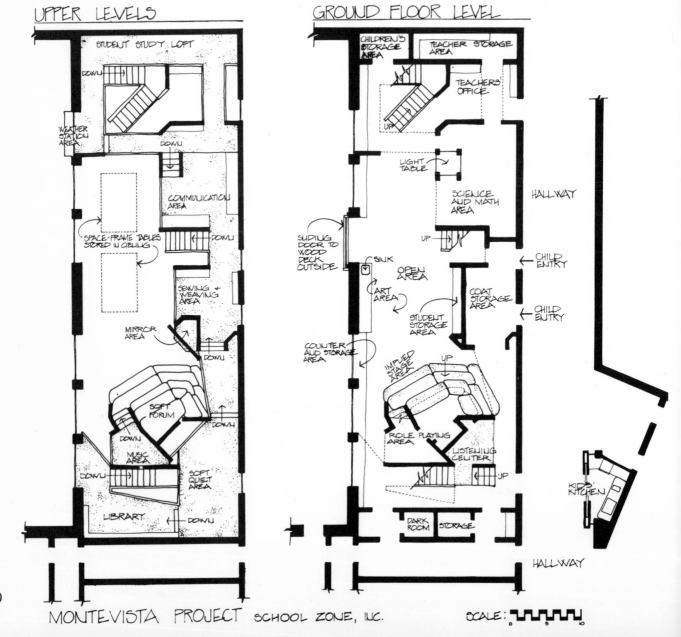

UPPER LEVELS

STUDENT STUDY LOFT
DOWN
WEATHER STATION AREA
DOWN
COMMUNICATION AREA
SPACE-FRAME TABLES STORED IN CEILING
DOWN
SEWING + WEAVING AREA
MIRROR AREA
DOWN
SOFT FORUM
DOWN
MUSIC AREA
DOWN
SOFT QUIET AREA
LIBRARY
DOWN

GROUND FLOOR LEVEL

CHILDREN'S STORAGE AREA
TEACHER STORAGE AREA
TEACHERS' OFFICE
UP
LIGHT TABLE
SCIENCE AND MATH AREA
HALLWAY
UP
SLIDING DOOR TO WOOD DECK OUTSIDE
SINK
OPEN AREA
CHILD ENTRY
ART AREA
COAT STORAGE AREA
STUDENT STORAGE AREA
CHILD ENTRY
COUNTER AND STORAGE AREA
IMPLIED STAGE AREA
UP
ROLE PLAYING AREA
LISTENING CENTER
UP
KIDS' KITCHEN
DARK ROOM
STORAGE
HALLWAY

70

MONTEVISTA PROJECT SCHOOL ZONE, INC.

SCALE:

Transition Area for Creative Learning

A transition area is a space between the indoor classroom and the playground. It is an area that is usually found just outside the doors and walls of a school building. It is dependent upon functions both in and outside the classroom.

In a traditional school setting, the transition area between inside and outside has simply been a threshold and a door. Today, a host of learning possibilities can be incorporated into the area immediately outside the entry to a classroom. These can include livestock pens, places for large-scale art activities, an extended classroom space, nature study and planting activities, a weather station, or even simply a place to stretch one's body and perhaps emit a frustrated yelp.

The transition space is not as permanent as the walls and ceiling of the indoor classroom, but it is much more dynamic. This space is influenced by the weather, the climate of a region, and even the time of day and the position of the sun. The activities that take place within this area should be planned to take advantage of the dynamics which surround the space. Passive or active activities that happen just outside the classroom walls act as a buffer for more active outdoor play.

A transition area between classroom and playground provides added space for learning experiences. An area with a southern exposure can be used for most of the year.

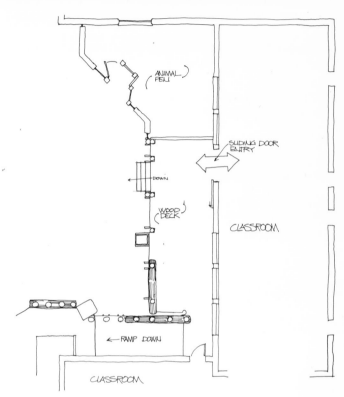

Multilevel plan to an open classroom with two teachers and fifty-five children. Notice how a hallway is used for a kitchen area. The enclosed area by the stairwell meets fire regulations.

4. DESIGNING OUTDOOR LEARNING ENVIRONMENTS

Traditionally, equipment installed on playground areas have indicated the kinds of amusements in which children might indulge. But are playgrounds as such beneficial? We question the legitimacy of their intended function. There is something almost inhumane about the idea of designating isolated areas where children may "play" without interfering in the presumably more important affairs of adults. There is something equally suspect in the notion that such areas are conveniences for children to work off their apparently frustrated energies. Has the massive installment of such standardized mechanical contrivances as swings, jungle gyms, and seesaws on these precious spaces served even that function well? Playgrounds are universally attached to schools, yet they have been consistently excluded from any curricular function, save for a few physical education provisions. Nowhere, in the traditional definitions of a playground, is education mentioned. We feel, however, that connecting the educational classroom environment to the playground would add new dimensions to both.

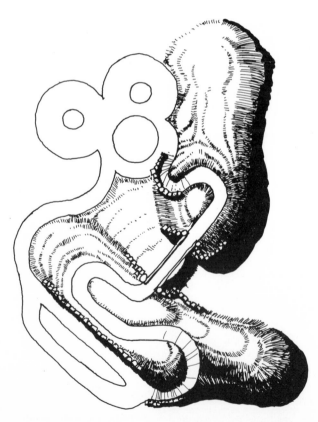

The alternative to the barren playgrounds dotting the American landscape would combine visual interest with physical challenge. Good playgrounds stimulate multisensory play. Landscape design for children is as important as park design for adult recreation.

72

The Playground as an Extension of the Classroom

The notion that a school's educational responsibility takes place only inside the building is outdated, and the degree of specialization attached to school building interiors must be broken down. We would like to show how the learning process may be expanded onto the school playground area in order to redefine the scope of a school facility as a teaching apparatus. Every inch of its property should be used for the purpose of education, for play is indeed a significant part of education—it is a child's work. As play environments provide more choices of activity and more natural and comfortable conditions, "play" becomes more vital, more sophisticated, and more effective as expression, whether it is constructive or relaxing. Principals and teachers who watch children on revitalized playgrounds tell us that discipline problems and vandalism decrease, and cooperation increases.

And yet, the yards are the more neglected areas of a school complex. Playgrounds seem to be placed on them as an afterthought. Most school budgets do not include playground development provisions, but even aside from the problem of cost, the playground is not an easy design project.

Most people who design playgrounds have little or no background in child development; generally their misconceived safety measures make for sterile settings. Aerial views of communities from one end of the country to another, in both urban and rural areas, present bald patches near schools, those recreation complexes that are immediately identifiable as playgrounds. One can almost detect the grids of paved surfaces with their minimal space standards of seventy-five square feet per child, enclosed by the ever-present chain-link fence.

Even the most "advantaged" children today, whose homes are stocked with toys and other diversions, are suffering from the deficiency of poor play environments. Playgrounds near schools are usually very large, with the exception of those in inner cities. Planners have neglected the power of creative outdoor spaces, although there is acreage potential waiting to be discovered all over this country. It is this abused outdoor setting that may be the saving grace for the educational system and the community which supports the school. By reshaping the learning potential of the playground, activities found in an entire neighborhood could be used for a community park as a nucleus for fun, play, and learning.

The school is a microcosm. The world can be reflected throughout the school and playground so that the child is confronted with a wide spectrum of real learning situations and is equipped with survival skills that stem from reality as well as from fantasy. A school should be a place where children want to be rather than a place where they have to be. In order to achieve this quality of education, people must rethink the very nature of children's play. They also need to learn how outdoor spaces can facilitate a child's development more fully by stimulating him to more creative thought and activity throughout his young career.

The playground should not be thought of as an exercise yard to be used at a specified time of the day, but as an extension of the classroom. It should be organized in very much the same manner: There can be interest centers, large group activity areas, complex traffic patterns, small passive areas, and large game fields. Children should be able to use the outdoors for learning.

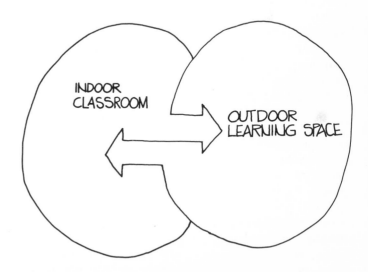

The playground should not be thought of as an exercise yard to be used at one specific time of the day, but as an extension of the classroom.

One of the many reasons children have been regulated in their access to the outdoors is the design of the school building. In order for children to go outdoors, each student has to leave the room, enter a central corridor, walk past several other classrooms, and open a large door with heavy hardware. In the process, he has had to open and shut two doors, disturb several classrooms with the echo of his footsteps throughout the halls, and walk some fifty yards to the playground. The idea of free-flowing or random access to the playground is simply impossible in this setting because the rooms do not have direct access to the outdoors.

Barriers to the outdoors exist with or without walls. Even schools with immediate access to the outdoors do not always allow their students to wander outside on a random basis because of the rigid recess schedule imposed on the daily routine.

This need not be so. The playground could be designed and organized as a teaching tool by giving the young students a reason to go outside. Once a playground has areas designed for special interests and needs, the experience-centered concept can be extended to the school yard. Outdoor learning experiences can consist of many activities, especially where the climate is mild for the greater part of the year. A ceramic pavilion, a wood shop, a greenhouse, a garden area, an animal pen, a game area, an outdoor amphitheater, and a weather station are just some of the many possibilities for outdoor learning.

To go outdoors in a traditional school, each student has to leave the room, use a central corridor, and then open a large door with heavy hardware. In the process, he has disturbed several classrooms and walked some fifty yards to the playground.

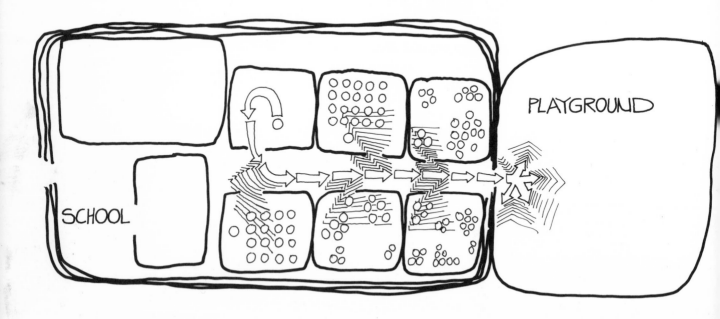

74

OUTDOOR LEARNING CENTERS

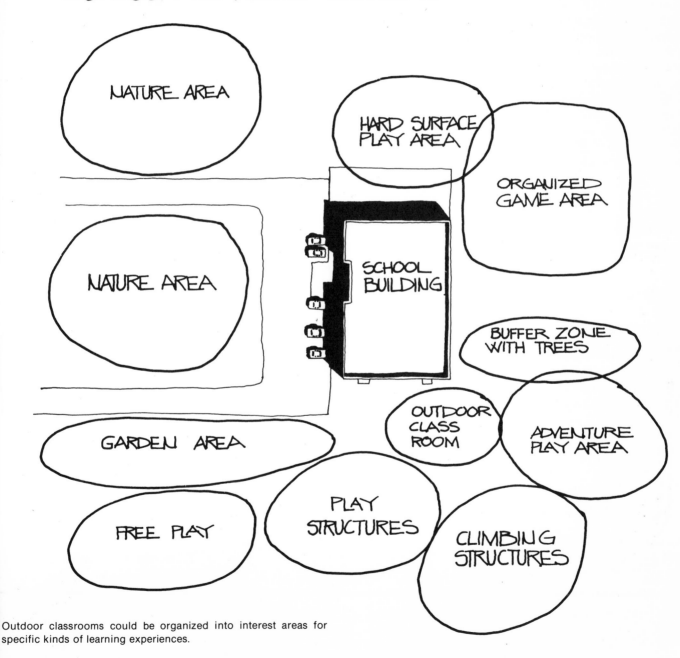

Outdoor classrooms could be organized into interest areas for specific kinds of learning experiences.

Community Playground Planning

When a school decides to create an innovative playground, the people responsible for the new design must evaluate how the space is to be used. Parents as well as teachers should be consulted; they need to analyze the children's play and, of course, the child himself needs to show us how he plays. Parents have traditionally been excluded from schools except in token ways such as the PTA and such social festivities as school carnivals or field trips.

In several workshops with a variety of parents and teachers, discussions revealed that parents do want to be a part of their children's education. They want to help decide what is to be taught and to actively participate in the learning process with their own children. The problem is that there is no vehicle for this parent participation in many of our schools; moreover, teachers and principals are threatened by their presence. One very useful and pleasant vehicle for parent involvement is playground planning and construction. The process outlined here applies to all kinds of playground development, whether a contractor does the work or not, since it is in the low-budget category and is within the financial reach of everyone.

People can get involved in several different ways:
1. Raising money.
2. Donating materials.
3. Volunteering labor and skill.
4. Using influence and contacts in the community for **supplies** and expertise.

Playground Planning Meetings

An assumption is made that the combined energies of many people collaborating on a problem-solving project (sometimes called "synergism") brings a more dynamic solution than if only one or two people work at it. A sample meeting schedule is described here to demonstrate the playground planning process.

Meeting One: Organization—People interested in doing something about their school playground should get together. Find an interested architect, one or more architectural students, or a parent with design expertise who might give you more planning advice, and organize yourself into a committee. (Also, many universities have community design centers.) Involve the principal and other school district administrators. Decide generally what it is you want to do.

Children can help to plan playgrounds. They can give adults a lot of information about their needs and what they would like. Adults need to observe children in play before they design for them.

Meetings Two, Three, and Four: Examination of How Children Play and the Area to be Used—Begin to examine what constitutes play; is play educational or is it recreational? What kinds of activities do children engage in on any playground? Brainstorm and write down the kinds of behavior that are named. Children run, jump, skip, bounce, swing, splash, roll, climb, push, pull, slide, sit, play with sand, etc. The range of activity will vary from very active to quiet and passive play.

On a continuum from active to passive play, there needs to be a balance of design for a convenient outdoor gathering place, for loitering, for wandering, and for passive watching without participation. Yet within this diversity, immediate and spontaneous conversation across all activities should be possible.

Ask for the school blueprints and look carefully at the playground's assets and liabilities. Analyze it in terms of the following considerations:

1. What is this playground to the school? Is it used only during school hours, and locked up after hours?

2. Does it have potential as a community playground or park to be used after school hours or at night during the summer?

3. Observe natural phenomena on the playground. What is the prevailing wind? Are there dust problems? Are there mud problems? Is there a sun problem? Are there any trees for shade? Are there any hills or multilevel areas for active running, or is your playground on a flat plane? Are there areas for gardens? Where is the water supply?

4. Consult with a physical-education person. What design criteria for the playground landscape can be extrapolated from the curriculum of "movement education," a new concept in body awareness and physical development?

In planning your playground, begin by sketching some ideas on paper so that discussion and design are taking place simultaneously.

Make a list of the things you would like to see on your playground. (Photo by Dan Aiello)

Meeting Five: Interview Children
1. What do they like best about school?
2. What do they do on the playground?
3. Where do the girls play?
4. Where do the boys play?
5. Do they ever play together?
6. What would they like to see on their playground that isn't there now?
7. Would they like to help take care of an animal pen, a garden, or a greenhouse?
8. What do they do after school between the hours of 3:30 PM and 8:30 the next morning?

Younger children have different environmental needs from older children because of the differences in motor skills, mental development, and physical size. These different scale and skill determinants act as subtle barriers between younger and older children. There can also be common areas such as amphitheaters, animal pens, and large playing fields where the varying age groups can come together and socialize.

Children should take part in the design and construction of the playground. During the construction process they can give useful criticism and help.

Consideration of the child's size should be very much a part of playground design. A variety of physical tasks ranging from simple to complex can challenge the child as he grows in physical stature and strength.

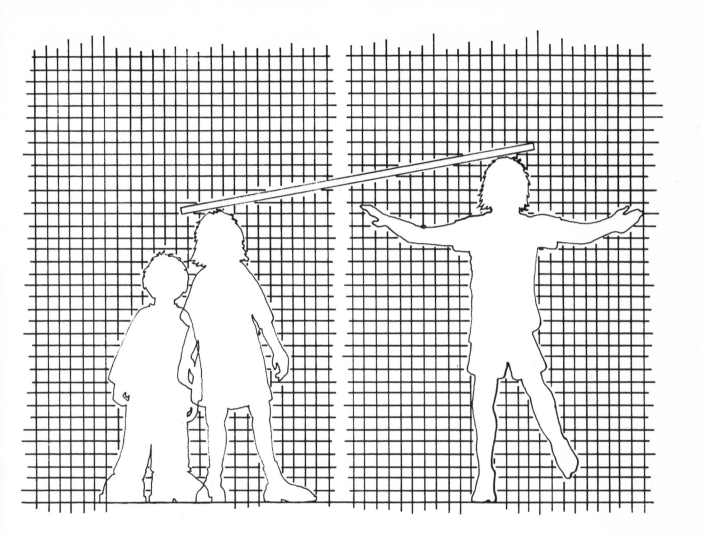

Meetings Six through Ten: Finalize Plans

1. Put a diagram of your playground on a wall surface and begin to think aloud, using graphic symbols.

2. Parents, teachers, and other community people should get up and draw suggestions on the diagrams. Brainstorm *what* should be on the playground and *where*, based on the information gathered in previous meetings. Each person should be able to give specific information on facts with which he has become intimately familiar. Ask parents to remember what was their favorite place to play as a child.

3. Finalize plans. How should the earth be shaped? Will there be play pits or mounds? What kind of level changes will there be? How will they be constructed? Is there to be grass? What kind of fencing or wall is going to be built? Where do the play structures go? Where are they? Will there be large playing fields or basketball courts?

4. Decide which items have priority. Make a sequential plan from large to smaller tasks, and organize them on a calendar. Decide which part of the playground will be developed first. It is a good idea to begin with spaces near the building and then gradually move out to the larger areas.

5. Build a model.

During the construction of a playground, the children's behavior immediately changes once there is a hole with a hill to climb. It is more challenging than level ground.

Earth mounds and play pits are fine play structures. They offer an easy way to create level changes on a playground. Be sure to design for efficient water drainage.

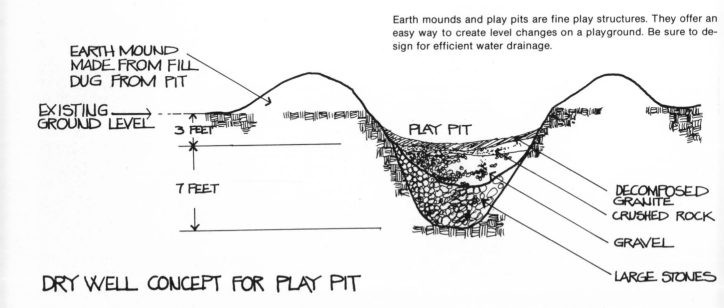

EARTH MOUND MADE FROM FILL DUG FROM PIT

EXISTING GROUND LEVEL

3 FEET

7 FEET

PLAY PIT

DECOMPOSED GRANITE

CRUSHED ROCK

GRAVEL

LARGE STONES

DRY WELL CONCEPT FOR PLAY PIT

6. A committee should be formed throughout the designing and building process to collect materials from the community. Materials should include a backhoe, tools, railroad ties, telephone poles, large rocks, old lumber, tree stumps, gravel, sand, grass seed, plants, trees, tires, cable spools, and cement culverts.

7. Identify resources in the community that can be tapped to help on this project.

8. A nearby military installation or industrial plant with a community service branch can help to survey; run a backhoe for earth digging and mounding; haul railroad ties on flatbed trucks (in the West, ties are lying by the tracks waiting to be picked up); provide labor.

There is a direct correlation between community and parent energy, and the amount of materials gathered for playground construction.

9. Assess the community and parent energy (we call it "sweat equity"). Is there a nursery nearby? Is there a parent with a construction firm? Are there parents who are bricklayers, plumbers, or electricians? Are there older children at the school or high school students who could get credit for work experience in building the playground?

10. Make detailed plans of weekend workshops and construction schedules. Have some parents arrange to provide food for the workers. (We've found that food is a great relaxant and that a lot of communication takes place when people are eating.)

Food is a come-on for community inspired playgrounds, and a necessary element in all-day work sessions.

Work Schedule and Tools

Here's a schedule you might follow in planning and working on your playground:

1. Stake out the playground area to be improved.
2. Take a core sample of earth, if necessary, to determine the kind of ground you are digging, or where the water table is.

The school chalk marker is used to make a giant blueprint of the playground design so that it is understandable to both the layman and the professional.

The district maintenance and operations crew take a core sample to determine the water table level.

3. Start ground shaping and mounding earth.
4. Dig trenches for walls, footings, electricity, and plumbing.
5. Put in steel reinforcement bars for footings and walls.
6. Pour footings.
7. Build walls.

Children are encouraged to help with simple and "safe" construction jobs.

The Albuquerque Public Schools believed in a prototype project. They lent their support to its completion.

Some playground construction might have to be done by profes-
sionals to insure safe structures.

The author tries her hand at stabilizing block walls. Professional
and lay people can work side by side.

There is a definite sequence in playground design from heavy tasks to finer ones.

Children learn how adobe walls are screened and plastered.

8. Begin play structures and banking of the earth with railroad ties, telephone poles, wooden spools, steel barrels, rocks, or whatever can be found.

9. Continue shaping the earth by hand. This is a long and tedious job.

10. Begin the structure (deck or walkways) that forms the transition area from inside the school building to the outside.

11. Install lights, drinking fountains, or other needed electrical outlets.

Try to seek out new and aesthetically pleasing ways to use found materials.

Construction of the amphitheater.

Energy and responsibility are shared, as in a family.

Detail of a textured area on a well-trafficked hill.

Playground equipment can be made from found materials.

12. Begin and complete such structures as play towers, amphitheaters, sand pits, slides, playhouses, water play area, seesaws, caves, jumping pit, picnic tables, benches, basketball courts, shade ramadas, swings (can be made from tires), tire bounce, suspension bridge.

(Photo by Larry Licht)

(Photo by Larry Licht)

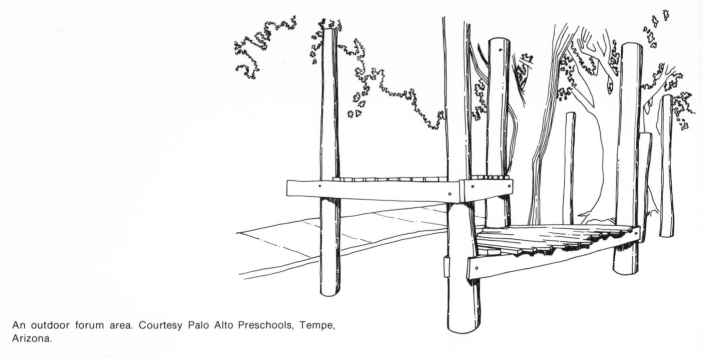

A simple deck under a tree.

An outdoor forum area. Courtesy Palo Alto Preschools, Tempe, Arizona.

Shade structure.

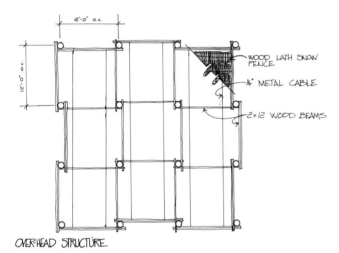

WOOD LATH SNOW FENCE
¼" METAL CABLE
2×12 WOOD BEAMS

OVERHEAD STRUCTURE

¼" METAL CABLE
2×12 BEAM
½" GARAGE BOLTS
TELEPHONE POLE

ELEVATION

A parent works on construction of the shade structure.

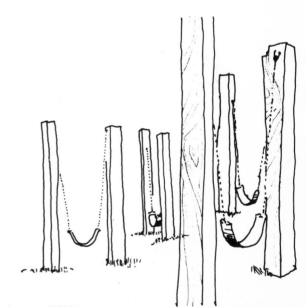

Swing possibilities.

91

13. Bring in top soil and tamp it down.

14. Plant grass and trees.

15. Watch your energies come alive through the children who use your well-designed playground.

Following is a list of tools you may have to rent or borrow: post-hole digger, bolt cutter, pipe bender, chain saw, earth tamper, shovels, wheelbarrows, backhoe, trench digger, welding equipment, table saw, heavy drill, hand tools, wire or cable stretcher, rebar cutter, a two-ton truck and a flatbed truck for heavy hauling.

The same planning steps can be used where there is a higher budget project and the work load is assumed by a contractor rather than volunteer help.

Play sculpture and private spaces. Courtesy Nueva Day School, Hillsborough, California.

A play labyrinth among the trees. Courtesy Nueva Day School, Hillsborough, California.

92

A city playground with brick textures. Courtesy Educational Facilities Laboratories. (Photo by Nancy Rudolph)

Alternative Scrounge for Playgrounds

Our present "garbage" culture, with its quantity of throwaway items, has provided us with a number of design possibilities that utilize found materials. Once these materials are found, they can be redefined, changed, and used in a variety of ways for play equipment, banking earth, fences, and other educational tools. Here are a number of such ideas for a playground.

Railroad ties are available from the railroads, especially at times when they may be replacing tracks, or ties, or both. Longer ties are more difficult to obtain because there is a new machine that cuts them out in three- and four-foot sections. (For information, call the station master in the city nearest you. You must have a permit from him in order to pick up ties next to tracks.)

Ties can be set vertically to berm up earth mounds, surface rough wear areas, and as structural members or fences. They can be used horizontally as walkways, as edging for planter beds and gardens, and as part of other textures.

Telephone poles are becoming difficult to find, but check with local utility companies. Some communi-

Part of the Monte Vista School outdoor learning classroom.

ties are replacing telephone poles with underground utilities, which could mean a bonanza for playground construction.

Find out if any poles have been abandoned in your area. Organize an early-morning parent group, rent a chain saw, and chop your own. Or, if you have the money, arrange to buy a truckload. They can be used as post and lintel support for climbing structures, as shade pavilions or ramadas, as decks, as supports for suspension bridges, as totem poles for children to carve or paint on, and for holding earth which steps from higher to lower levels.

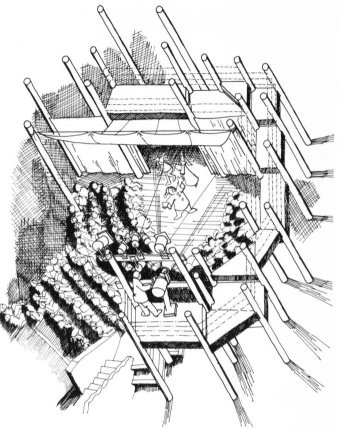

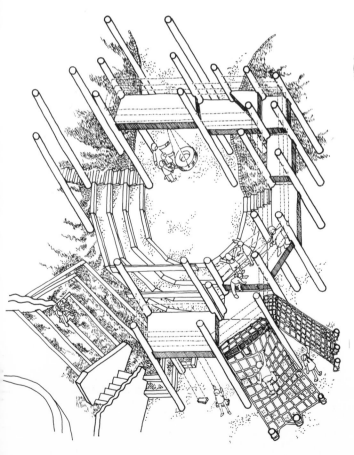

Designing for multiple uses creates a more flexible environment. These two schematic designs show a climbing structure that can also become an amphitheater and drama center. This is all possible with contoured land, adobe and cinder block walls, telephone poles, wood platforms, and fabric.

Utility companies will give away wooden cable spools. Quite often we see them plunked down in playgrounds, used as they are. They can also be ripped apart and used in other ways as a rolling toy, a chair, as a walkway, and as sections for a bridge.

Cement culverts or old oil drums are excellent devices for a tunnel. The drums need to be welded. Older children could help to make a sculpture. Cement culverts, heavy as they may be, are frequently used in playgrounds. If they are integrated with earth mounds or are covered with dirt, or act as a tunnel through a mound, they are less obtrusive and more a part of an organic landscape plan than if they are left sitting above ground.

We observed how some children used cable spools—as a rolling experience! Once a few boards were removed, a child crawled into the center of the spool; the other students then pushed the spool about. This gave us the idea of movable playground equipment.

Cable spool rocking-rolling chair. (Design by George Vlastos)

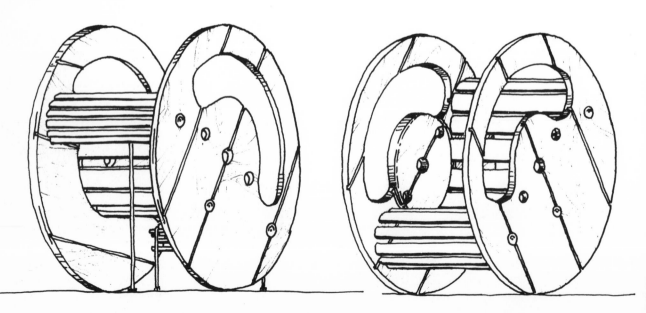

SUSPENSION BRIDGE
MADE FROM TELEPHONE POLES
AND HEAVY ROPE.

Suspension bridge for the Monte Vista School project. The suspension bridge builds balance skills. It moves as the child crosses it, requiring a high degree of psychomotor skill development.

Children tell us they desire personal space, even on the playground. (Photo by Larry Licht)

Roof tiles make good drainage or irrigation ditches. The terra-cotta can break easily, so they need to be set into cement.

Caring about birds and learning about their contribution to our ecosystem is important. Bird feeders can be made a number of different ways, and children can make wooden ones themselves. If you can find any old pan-shaped discs (from discing farm machinery), add a chain and you have an excellent bird feeder. Hang it near a window for easy viewing and maintenance.

Old tree stumps make excellent climbing and balancing structures. Sawed-off sections of trees can be used for steps or walkways and can be placed at different heights and widths for physical development play.

Tires have been commonly used in playground renovation for tire bounces, attached to poles for soft climbers, filled with sand for sand play, and as swings.

Palisades Swimming Club Playground, Glen Echo, Maryland. Tree sections make excellent balance beams too. Courtesy Educational Facilities Laboratories. (Photo by George Zimbel)

Some Brainstorming on Other Playground Features

1. Set aside a small area of the playground and include a selection of junk for children to use, under supervision, for construction projects. Include tires, lumber, hammers, nails, old doors, rope, paint, cable spools, and dirt.

2. Include props for expressive play.

3. Commission an artist, perhaps with the help of your local arts council, to build a play sculpture.

4. Build a maze.

5. Build a tricycle track with a variety of surfaces: bricks, cobblestones, aggregate concrete (bumpy), cement (smooth), wavy, straight, wide, narrow, and zigzag.

6. Let the school grounds reflect the fact that children live there. In constructing pathways or gardens, let children bring their own treasures and embed them in cement, or make their own handprints a part of the design—a privilege usually reserved for movie stars.

7. Build a shaded place for adults to sit.

8. Construct a graffiti wall for children to paint on. A graffiti wall on the school grounds lets the public know that children have something to say and are very imaginative in saying it. It allows for human expression, and it can be whitewashed or painted over so that it is a constantly changing surface.

This graffiti wall tells the community that children live here. In painting the wall, children learn something about scale and enlargement, and they have a good time negotiating the scaffolding.

Schools should reflect the fact that they are for children. A discovery garden with children's hand prints or the small shells that they have contributed, helps children have a sense of belonging. (Photo by Dan Aiello)

9. Make a compost pile or methane-gas container for gardening purposes or for producing other forms of energy. (Methane gas is a by-product of decomposed animal wastes and is an ignitable cooking gas.) A compost bin is easy to construct and can be made from wood, fencing material, brick, or rocks. Instead of wasting food, children can learn about recycling and can get used to the habit of saving.

10. Build a solar-energy greenhouse to teach a child concepts about botany, the scientific method, and alternative-energy systems. Solar collectors could be built too.

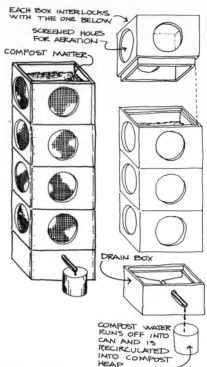

A CONCEPT FOR A MODULATED COMPOST SYSTEM BY SCHOOL ZONE INC.

EACH BOX INTERLOCKS WITH THE ONE BELOW

SCREENED HOLES FOR ABRATION

COMPOST MATTER

DRAIN BOX

COMPOST WATER RUNS OFF INTO CAN AND IS RECIRCULATED INTO COMPOST HEAP

Modular composting system. (Design by George Vlastos)

A methane-gas producer along with a composting system gives children experience with ecosystems.

MINI-METHANE-GENERATOR SCHEMATIC BY SCHOOL ZONE INC.

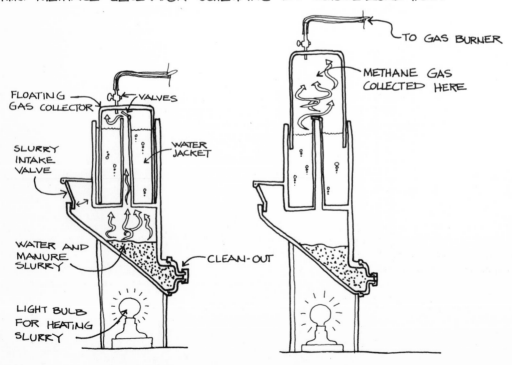

TO GAS BURNER

METHANE GAS COLLECTED HERE

FLOATING GAS COLLECTOR

VALVES

WATER JACKET

SLURRY INTAKE VALVE

WATER AND MANURE SLURRY

CLEAN-OUT

LIGHT BULB FOR HEATING SLURRY

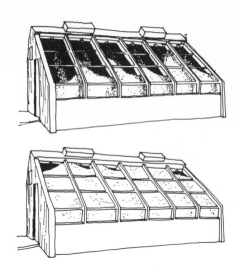

Solar-energy greenhouse. (Design by Zomeworks)

AT SUN SET BEADS OF INSULATION ARE FORCED INTO THE PANELS TO CONTAIN THE SOLAR ENERGY GENERATED DURING THE DAY.

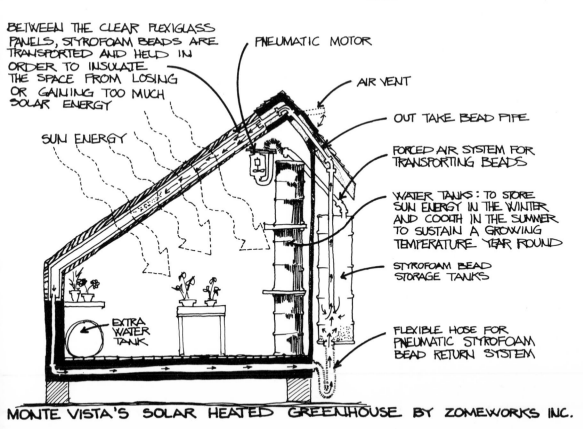

BETWEEN THE CLEAR PLEXIGLASS PANELS, STYROFOAM BEADS ARE TRANSPORTED AND HELD IN ORDER TO INSULATE THE SPACE FROM LOSING OR GAINING TOO MUCH SOLAR ENERGY

SUN ENERGY

PNEUMATIC MOTOR

AIR VENT

OUT TAKE BEAD PIPE

FORCED AIR SYSTEM FOR TRANSPORTING BEADS

WATER TANKS: TO STORE SUN ENERGY IN THE WINTER AND COOLTH IN THE SUMMER TO SUSTAIN A GROWING TEMPERATURE YEAR ROUND

STYROFOAM BEAD STORAGE TANKS

EXTRA WATER TANK

FLEXIBLE HOSE FOR PNEUMATIC STYROFOAM BEAD RETURN SYSTEM

MONTE VISTA'S SOLAR HEATED GREENHOUSE BY ZOMEWORKS INC.

11. Every school ought to have some form of windmill, to generate electricity, or to pump water, perhaps to irrigate some part of the barren playground. (Many towns are situated on streams which used to have water wheels for grinding grain; utilization of an old mill by the school could give children a better lesson in history than any textbook.)

Children and plants complement each other in a very natural way.

Cactus

Because they have nurtured life, watched and charted its growth, felt the warmth of solar energy, and understood the mechanism of the greenhouse, first graders now understand many new concepts.

12. Build a tree house.

13. Use painted garbage cans.

14. Hang climbing ropes.

15. Keep modular toys stored nearby so that the supervisor can distribute them.

16. Build an amphitheater or an outdoor classroom.

17. Build a musical fence or screen with a variety of textures that can be rubbed with a stick to produce a variety of tonal qualities.

18. Build a suspension bridge.

19. Hang unbreakable mirrors.

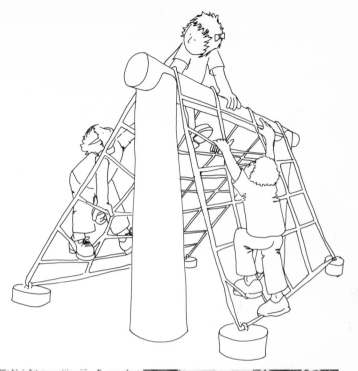

Using ship ropes from a salvage yard lets children delineate their own climbing structure. (Photo by Larry Licht)

20. Include a boat (for real water, or pretend).
21. Include an old tree trunk.
22. Build a child-scaled play pit.
23. Have seeds for an herb garden on hand.
24. Build a cable ride on a pulley system.
25. Include a flat surface for games.

Palisades Swimming Club Playground, Glen Echo, Maryland. Courtesy Educational Facilities Laboratories. (Photo by George Zimbel)

If people in a neighborhood really want a playground they can have one. These before and after photos show a small space and what was accomplished with it. Courtesy Educational Facilities Laboratories.

26. Include educational play structures designed to teach concepts. Here are some examples of recreational equipment that incorporate selected scientific and mathematical principles in their design: a zome (a climbing structure which teaches geometry and architecture); a pressure tank fountain; a möbius-strip jungle gym; an inverse-square jungle gym; a pythagorean wading pool; an underground room or tunnel for study of burrowing animals; solar collectors; a weather station.

Detail of the Zomework climber.

From this basic form, children can design the climbing structures that appeal to them. (Design by Zomeworks)

PYTHAGOREAN WADING POOL

PRESSURE TANK FOUNTAIN

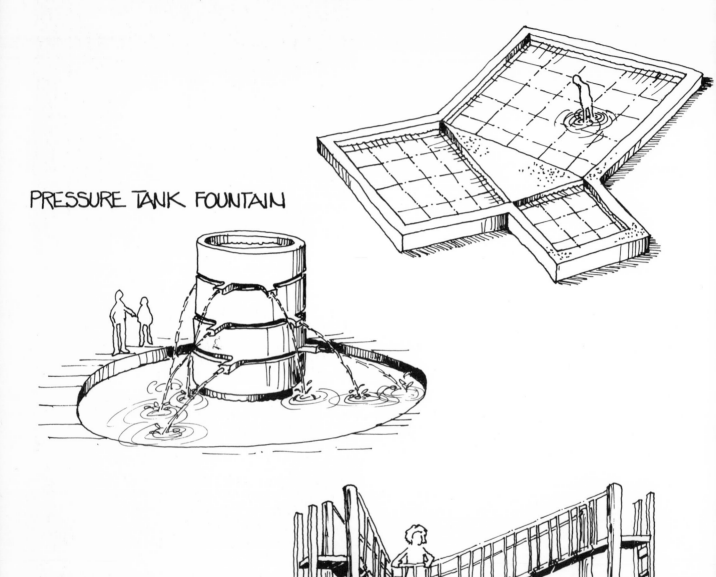

CATENARY CURVE BRIDGE

INVERSE SQUARE TUNNEL GYM

Movement and learning balance are very much a part of a young child's growth. They should also play a role in playground design.

Play is the way children learn about themselves and the world around them. Play environments, like any learning environment, must be rich in multisensory stimuli to foster imagination, personality, growth, and physical capability. Play environments can be created anywhere. In summary, we have tried to show how school playgrounds can be enriched and changed to provide for meaningful recreation.

Solutions to design problems offered in this chapter are presented only as part of our ongoing environmental research. They are experimental solutions and we are still asking many questions about them. The energy of many people can offer new and varied designs to educational problems. Community-based answers are the best because the process itself is a vibrant example of democratic communication.

Courtesy Santa Clara Pueblo, New Mexico.

Cultural elements and vernacular architecture can be part of the playground too. This playhouse is made of rocks from a sacred ancestral dwelling. Courtesy Santa Clara Pueblo, New Mexico.

Ridge Hill Elementary School. Courtesy Educational Facilities Laboratories. (Photo by George Zimbel)

5. HOW TO WORK IN AN OPEN CLASSROOM

To simply provide teachers and children with a rich environmental setting is not enough. We are so used to thinking of the school as a cold institution with all kinds of rules that we have overlooked its potential for real involvement, commitment, and teaching. We know from our experience that children are better off in an enriched and well-provisioned setting because they respond to exciting stimuli, and, through their natural curiosity, discover information on their own. But much more can happen when the teacher is open to life herself and can use her environment as a support system for learning. Provocative questions asked of the seeking child can help to bring properties of the setting alive. Spontaneous experiences in the sand area, in the garden, at a weather station, or in the greenhouse alert the child's emotions and physical senses, which then mesh with thought processes. The teacher does not dispense knowledge but encourages, guides, and stimulates discussion, and thus motivates the child to more complex learning.

Provocative questions from an inquisitive child provide a reverse avenue for learning that is not found in traditional teacher-centered settings.

Characteristics of an Open Classroom

In an open classroom, learning is based on the current interests and needs of the children; in this way, they formulate the knowledge they wish to acquire on their own. The curriculum is largely spontaneous rather than determined in advance. The environment and materials for instruction are carefully chosen for specific purposes, and are orchestrated through a curriculum-organizing system, or an experience directory. The teacher has intimate knowledge of what is to be learned so that when moments of spontaneous interest arise she can help the child learn the basic principles of a body of knowledge. This necessitates a highly creative and flexible teacher. It also involves some practice and doesn't happen overnight.

In an open classroom, a child who spends all his time playing with blocks may be gaining experience with concepts of shape, structure, architectural balance, cantilevering, or strength. A child who likes to weave gets practice in counting and pattern perception. Some children have typical childlike interests, while others are interested in subjects such as architecture, anatomy, and botany that do not fit into the standard elementary school curriculum. Some children like taking short walking tours to examine fences in the neighborhood and to graph the number of each kind that they find. In this kind of classroom, pupils touch and manipulate real, concrete materials, and there is little reliance on completed worksheets or on making pupils listen and watch demonstrations. Learning can happen anywhere and with anybody. The janitor, the cook, the secretary, parents, as well as peers can teach. In order to accommodate the principle that children learn much faster from each other, groups of a variety of ages and abilities are commonly found in open schools.

Noise levels in open schools are much higher than those in regular schools, but the noise is productive because it is a result of the children's excitement about their work. The assessment of pupil progress is not by teacher-designed or standardized testing. A child is compared with himself and not with others. Anecdotal records and checklists of what a child can do show where he is in terms of capability. Assessing a child's knowledge and progress over time is a part of the evaluation.

Teachers must be creative in their use of the environment as a teaching tool. A walking trip through the neighborhood can be a potent learning experience.

Understanding involves communication. Courtesy Pacific Oaks College. (Photo by Gail Ellison Milder)

Open classroom educators accept the notion that children must acquire a thorough elementary school knowledge of reading, writing, arithmetic, and other disciplines. Although open schools introduce many new areas of knowledge into their curricula, they continue to emphasize the child's acquisition of basic knowledge in language arts and mathematics. Parents insist upon this. But other objectives are also recognized as valid. One child may wish to spend his time playing with and acquiring information about snakes, another may informally work at gaining knowledge of geometric shapes, through block play, while a third child may be painting pictures. All are recognized forms of specialized knowledge and are valid educational objectives.

If all these activities are to happen simultaneously, it is obvious that a rich, ever-changing learning environment is a must.

The child interacts with a tangible environment, which teaches him by helping him to teach himself. We know that the change from a traditional classroom to open education is not something that happens in a year. But, for perhaps the first time in our history, we have an opportunity to promote children's responsibility for their own actions, and thus to impart to them more effectively the very ideals of our democratic society.

Confidence, initiative, and responsibility are among those personal traits we wish most to nurture in our children as they approach adult life. We have recently seen a great need to help children distinguish between freedom and license.

The open classroom concept looks to parents and community members as valuable resource people—they are frequent classroom participants. Open teachers are not threatened by their presence and see them as welcome additions, as individuals who have a lot to offer children. Parents are welcome to take part in woodworking, cooking, sewing, growing plants and planning gardens, listening to children read, sharing personal work, and talking with children. This last is especially valuable in schools where parents speak the native language of the predominant population. They have precious gifts to give children. We should set up special avenues of entry into schools for these people who, in the past, may have felt like intruders in an academic setting.

Parents insist that children acquire basic skills and knowledge. New environments and new teaching methods provide more of a challenge to children than those of their parents' day. We need to educate parents about the value of the new methodologies.

Other educational objectives for children are valid too. Survival skills are not always learned in a formal setting.

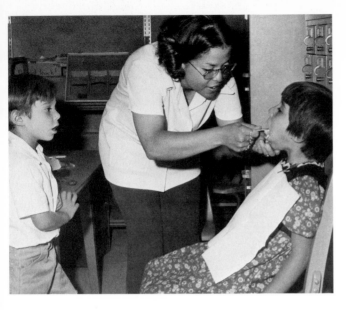

A move away from the structured classroom is not exactly a comforting proposition. Many children in traditional classrooms quickly learn to escape authoritarian pressures by hiding behind their desks. There are no such hiding places in the open classroom; but, as children in this setting must frequently work out in the open with each other, they soon learn to deal with mistake and failure as common phenomena rather than as measures of worth. Children need to know that it is in fact admirable to try something new, at the risk of failure, in front of others.

The open classroom method looks to parents and community members as valuable resource people.

Open teachers are not threatened by community members.

In open classrooms children work in an open fashion. Mistakes and failure are common phenomena rather than measures of worth.

Setting up Experience Centers

If complete architectural overhaul is not feasible, it is possible to set up some simple experience centers. Such centers include math, art, cognitive and psychomotor games, dramatic play, block play, housekeeping, library, writing, science, sand play, water play, and woodworking.

More complicated experience centers that might be used by the whole school include a mechanic's garage and automobiles or airplanes; a greenhouse, or, especially in cities, a roof garden; a press installation for the printing of pamphlets or books; structure centers, like a geodesic dome, a tent or an inflatable; a mini-farm (or a real farm), built on the unused portion of the school playground, featuring small crops, livestock, and fruit trees; a boat for marine study and recreation projects; vacant or even quite active storefronts; darkrooms; audio and video studios for actual productions (many projects can be enhanced by use of equipment that often sits untouched in the storerooms of these studios); neighborhood churches, factories, planetariums, art museums, and studios.

Courtesy Educational Facilties Laboratories. (Photo by George Zimbel)

A simple reading work center was constructed of cardboard. Each design has symbolic meaning for the adult and for the child.

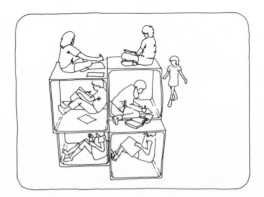

Four cubes can provide personal space, a climbing structure, or a role-playing area—a simple solution to the need for experience centers. In this case the children can make it become whatever they want.

Materials Selection

The selection of materials for experience centers should follow some of these guidelines:

1. Materials should be versatile for use in a variety of ways.

2. They should be self-explanatory and require a minimal number of instructions for use.

3. They should provide corrective feedback to children.

4. A material is useful if it helps the student to discover new and unfamiliar concepts.

5. Materials help young children to understand concepts on concrete manipulative levels rather than through words or pictures.

Seriation and other mathematical concepts can be taught with very simple materials. The key is the teacher. How well does he or she know what is to be taught so as to seize upon the moment for learning, and use the environment creatively? Educational Facilities Laboratories. (Photo by George Zimbel)

Manipulative materials must be carefully chosen and should foster curricular objectives.

The materials a teacher chooses are crucial to the learning that is expected to take place.

6. Materials should be multisensory.

7. "Open-ended" materials are useful so that a child can use his own maturity to work through them to higher forms of self-expression. Open-ended items such as art supplies, blocks, small manipulatives, writing paper, sand, and water lead to higher expressive levels and to the exchange of ideas between teachers and children.

8. Materials that produce an unexpected and incongruous result intrigue children and motivate them to resolve discrepancies.

Once experience centers are set up, it becomes a question of how to use them, and for what curricular goals. The teacher becomes a facilitator or a learning catalyst. This book is not intended to be a textbook on classroom management. But, if we can guide the classroom designer in developing a rich and ever changing environment, classroom instruction will be much easier.

Early Learning Center in Stamford, Connecticut. Many years ago, Maria Montessori, an Italian educator, discovered the value of rich multisensory materials for learning. Courtesy Educational Facilities Laboratories. (Photo by George Zimbel)

Courtesy Educational Facilities Laboratories. (Photo by Bob Perron)

An Experience Directory for Organizing Curriculum

As described in Chapter 2, there is a method for organizing curriculum which can help in the assembly of materials around themes of interest. This system is called an experience directory.

A major difference between an experience directory and other manifestations of open education is that it structures and equips the classroom with a system of topics known to be of interest to children. The topics are called "motivators" and include such well-established child interests as bones, birthdays, cowboys, highways, caves, trees, water, families, and friends. Unusual and exciting experiences related to each motivator are delineated. Through use of the experiences, the teacher helps children attain important objectives not likely to be accomplished by completing textbooks and holding workshops in the conventional classroom. These objectives include growth in cognitive reasoning abilities (toward more abstract concepts from classifying, sequencing, etc.); problem-solving and use of the scientific method; creativity and self-expression; divergent and evaluative thinking; enhanced self-esteem through recognition of the child's culture in school; enjoyment of learning by acknowledging the place of "romance" and "trivia" in the school curriculum (as described by Alfred North Whitehead in *The Aims of Education*).

In addition to the above, there is the objective of acquiring certain important content; but, unlike other curricula, this content can be acquired in an interdisciplinary fashion—what each motivator can yield in terms of mathematics, social studies, science, language arts, and other areas, is indicated. Fundamental principles from a particular discipline that are learned in association with one motivator are cross-referenced so that they can also be learned (or reviewed) in the context of another motivator. Cross-referencing of principles is an important educational feature of the experience directory organizing system since, in the elementary school years, a generalization or principle is only as broad and meaningful as the number of its examples that are available.

An important characteristic of the experiences suggested for each motivator is that they emphasize firsthand concrete involvement with materials, objects, and events. They typically include manipulation of collections of objects, walking trips into the community, experimentation with materials under varying conditions, dramatic role play, and cooking. These experiences replace the more common curricular activities in which knowledge is acquired vicariously through books, films, and other audio-visual media, or group activities specified and directed by a teacher. The rationale for the emphasis on firsthand experience is in keeping with the philosophy of open education. It is based on the well-documented findings from developmental and educational psychology that young children learn best by acting upon objects, and that such concrete experience is an essential prerequisite to more abstract and formal modes of acquiring information.

There is a very vital and practical reason for structuring the open classroom into a system of interrelated motivators, activities, and objectives. Open education as self-directed learning is an exciting idea, but it is almost impossible for the average classroom teacher. A successful open program demands an unusually skillful teacher who is always able to expand upon a child's interest at the appropriate time to help him acquire the skills, attitudes, knowledge, and abilities that he needs. Self-directed learning means that the teacher must invest a great deal of time in establishing favorable conditions for valid educational experiences to occur. Some of these activities may perhaps benefit and be performed by only a few of the many pupils. The burden on the teacher with twenty-five or more pupils, each with his own idiosyncratic interest, is enormous. However desirous the teacher may be of orienting the classroom program toward informal learning, he will probably fail *unless* he has a method for programing the diversity of children's interests while at the same time insuring that they continue to acquire basic skills, attitudes, and knowledge in the context of these interests.

The experience directory thus enables the teacher to successfully manage learning in an informal context. It provides a system of motivators and related activities to meet well-defined objectives. These motivators have been selected on the basis of two criteria—the well-established interests of children and cultural relevancy. With these criteria, it is highly likely that pupils will attend to one or several of these topics rather than to their more individual interests.

The program suggests numerous objectives to the teacher that can be obtained in relation to each motivator or interest, as well as unusual and exciting activities through which the objectives can be reached. Moreover, evaluation of pupil progress is specified for each experience in terms of these very objectives. This means of evaluation is of special importance since one of the common problems associated with enacting a program of open education has been the failure to define objectives and to relate pupil progress to those objectives.

Because the directory contains a constant set of objectives, constant kinds of experiences to which any theme of child interest can be applied, and a constant evaluation schema or feedback loop related to each objective, it is a generative system. And, although the experience directory is primarily intended to serve as a tool for instructional planning, it is also a methodology for teachers which will eventually enable them to independently devise their own worthwhile learning activities in response to any new interests expressed by their pupils.

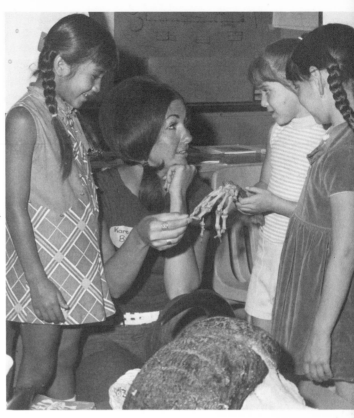

A collection of bones can lead children into archaeology, anatomy, science, cooking, math, art, music, and a variety of other interdisciplinary experiences.

119

Guide to Developing the Experience Directory

Anyone can use the following guide for setting up his own experience directory.

1. The first step is to list principles to be taught from all discipline areas at a given developmental level.

2. As stated in Chapter 2, know where principles are derived from more than one discipline.

3. Establish a list of themes of interest that can be used to convey these principles. You may want to make a cross-referenced index of principles and themes (a librarian can be of help). For example, here are some themes that we identified for southwestern children.

Bones
Barbed wire
Corn
Beans
Black cowboys
Park forest rangers
Animal doctors
Babies and old people (life and death)
Mud
Yarn
Santos
Southwestern toys and games
Kachina dolls
Cacti
Chili
Rocks and gems
Pottery and pottery sherds
Herbs and wild flowers
Mexican tin objects
Candlesticks
Gourds and rattles
Snakes and the snake dance
Bears
Insects
Horses
Sheep
The state fair
Medicine men
Mountain climbers
Highways
Trading posts
The chuck wagon
Adobe ovens
The combine machine
Pickup trucks
Jeeps
Church bells
The cottonwood tree
The piñon pine
The juniper bush
Rainstorms and desert floods
The fire dance
Saints' days
Birthdays, southwestern style
Fiestas
Southwestern Christmas

4. Take one theme and develop it to generate inter-disciplinary learning and a variety of experiences.

5. Know your resources across disciplines. Seek the help of a librarian or media specialist.

Theme

Principles to be Learned

Suggested Experiences

This format differs from traditional unit lesson planning in that it crosses all the disciplines and is experimentally oriented. For example, the chart on page 00 is a partial illustration of how we handled themes for the interest of corn. All principles to be learned and all suggested experiences have not been included, but the sample should give you ideas on how to develop your own themes.

5. Design an environment or a series of environments that will host experience directory learning. Gardens, cooking areas, a greenhouse, or a museum corner could all contribute to the intense study of corn, for example. The cooking environment is used here as an example of the possible learning experiences derived from such an experience center.

Learning as it Occurs in the Cooking Environment

A portable or a stationary cooking environment should contain the following equipment: sink, refrigerator, and stove with oven, a chopping block, and storage capabilities. This environment is designed to give children direct experience with active preparation of food in order to effect the educational outcomes listed below. Using cooking as a concrete experience can enhance interdisciplinary learning of principles and can further the communicative effectiveness of children.

Measurement, fractions, language development, art, and social development can all be brought out in a cooking environment.

A. Cultural education
 1. Differences and similarities of foods of various cultures. Foods associated with feast days, holidays, seasons and geographic areas.
 2. Preparation of food—varying kinds of preparation for the same foods.
 3. Cooking utensils and modes of cooking—historical and contemporary. Use materials from museum collections and contemporary cupboards.
 4. Types of ovens—gas, adobe, clay, underground. Appreciation and enjoyment of other cultures and how they prepare and preserve food.

B. Sensory, perceptual, and conceptual development
 1. Multisensory awareness of the various properties of food: sweet, sour, bitter, acid, soft, hard, cooked, uncooked, mushy, solid, liquid, gaseous (steam), cold, hot, etc. The many colors and shapes of food. Roasting, frying, baking, and boiling.

C. Language arts learning
 1. Learning to follow directions.
 2. Reading recipes will have meaning for the child because there will be concrete examples of the words being read.
 3. Learning to keep records.
 4. Verbalizing about substances, procedures, and events that the child experiences directly by preparing and tasting.
 5. Relating events in the sequence in which they occurred.
 6. Writing experience charts.
 7. Acquiring a more precise use of language.
 8. Enhanced skill in narration, explanation, and description.

D. Math learning
 1. Learning about measurement through the use of measuring spoons, cups, and scales.
 2. Experience with fractions through measurement.
 3. Experiencing the invariants of various shaped containers—round, oval, funnel, square, etc.—relating to geometry.
 4. Learning concepts of quantity, and the invariance of mass, weight, and volume despite changes in shapes.
 5. Experiencing and mathematically figuring the reduction and augmentation of recipes and the quantity of food.
 6. Concrete experiences with the above through such mathematic skills as addition, subtraction, division, and multiplication.
 7. Counting and estimating experience.
 8. Comprehending and using numerical terminology, for example, *most*, *none*, *few*, *as many as*.
 9. Alternative systems of measurement and the arbitrary basis of our system of measurement.

E. Science learning
 1. Awareness of the food chain.
 2. Learning about the changing state of food.
 3. Learning about fire and heat.
 4. Learning to read a thermometer.
 5. Gas heat vs. electricity.
 6. The technology of cooking—what makes it work.
 7. Thickening agents—flour, eggs, cornstarch—and how heat affects the food that they thicken.
 8. All about risers such as yeast, baking powder, air, heat.
 9. All about flavorings.
 10. How cold affects food and changes its state.
 11. All about the preservation of food through freezing and drying.
 12. How heat affects food and helps change its state.
 13. The recycling of garbage and composting.
 14. The changing state of matter.

Solar energy, often an abstract concept for young children, can come alive through the use of solar cooking.

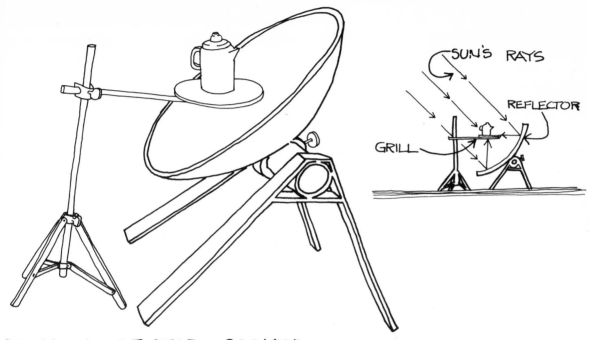

SOLAR REFLECTOR COOKER

FRESH BREAD

WELL DONE TOAST

The changing state of matter is easily understood through cooking.

A SIMPLE EXPERIMENT SHOWING A CHANGE OF STATE THROUGH COOKING.

F. Social studies learning
  1. Why do we eat what we eat.
  2. The various methods of food processing—canning, freezing, preserving.
  3. All about the geography of growing things and also about the effects of seasonal change.
  4. Some familiar foods and how various peoples cook them (beans, corn, pork, etc.)
  5. What happens to waste and garbage (recycling).
  6. The "route" food takes from its original source to the final product.
  7. Learning to maintain a compost pile to observe the changing state of matter.

G. Health and safety learning
  1. Why it is important to eat good food—food for survival.
  2. All about the simple concepts of nutrition.
  3. Learning to take responsibility for cooking utensils and machinery. The child will learn certain precautions and why they should be taken.
  4. Getting to know the proper use of knives, gas, and understanding safety regulations.
  5. Why it is important to maintain cleanliness and sanitation regulations.

H. Psychomotor development
  1. Pouring and measuring will facilitate eye-hand coordination which is related to early reading and writing capability.
  2. Use of knives for chopping will facilitate eye-hand coordination.
  3. Sewing aprons will also enhance eye-hand coordination.

I. Personality development and interpersonal relationships
  1. Cooking experiences can facilitate divisions of labor and cooperation and can demonstrate the productivity of the group. This is important because young children tend to work in parallel fashion rathan than *with* each other.
  2. Sharing.
  3. Peer group talking.
  4. Demonstration to other members of the group can facilitate complementary and symmetrical relationships between peers (communication objectives).
  5. Responsibility through performing clean-up activities.
  6. Pride of mastery with the learning of new techniques and skills.
  7. Opportunity for leadership.
  8. Devising group regulations and following them.
  9. Relating home culture to school learning and thus making minority group children feel more comfortable in school.
  10. Interacting creatively with the environment will enhance confidence in self.

J. Creative-aesthetic experiences
  1. Food as ornamentation—dyeing bean and melon seeds and then stringing them.
  2. Food as an art form. Decorative cooking—frosting cakes, braiding and cooking dough, making cutouts.
  3. Learning color concepts through use of food coloring and mixing colors, for example for frosting.
  4. Cooking as a stimulus and motivation for rhythmic, musical, and creative writing activities.
  5. Food as functional and decorative (dried chili peppers, dried Indian corn).
  6. Food as a subject matter source for artists. Show children still lifes and other paintings using food. Have children paint their own pictures of watermelons, fruit, vegetables and other food.

Learning Activities Related to the Cooking Environment

This is not a list of recipes, but a summary of worthwhile educational experiences revolving around the cooking environment. These experiences have more to do with the topics of heat and cold, ecology, food storage and preservation, mathematics, and dramatic play than they do with the actual preparing and cooking of foods.

Of course, you should also prepare and eat several foods. Simple foods are best and a limit of six to eight children at a time is advisable. Any cookbook will give you the recipes you want.

The Stove

A. Examining stoves
1. Take a trip to the cafeteria kitchen and to the teacher's lounge to examine the stove. Compare size, shape, color, and means of generating heat of both these stoves with the one in the cooking environment.
2. Talk about the stove as a single object. Possible vocabulary words to develop include, *counter height*, *knobs*, *buttons*, *handle*, *oven*, *pilot light*, *matches*, *timer*, *burner*, *grill*, *drip pan*, and *heating element*.
3. Before taking the children on this walking trip, have a preliminary talk with them to explore what they already know about stoves. See if they know what kind of cooking is done on top of a stove and in an oven. After the discussion has gone as far as the children can manage, take them to see stoves around the school.

B. Learning how heat changes things
1. Place a variety of substances in a hot oven— water, clay, bread, raisins, chili, plastic, glass, paper, butter, and a candle. Study and list the outcomes. Learn what evaporation means.
2. Visit a potter to examine a kiln and to look at pottery before and after it is fired.

C. To see that heat travels
1. Take a metal rod or tie a wire between two chairs. Affix a row of marbles to the wire with wax. Heat one end of the wire with a candle. The marbles drop off one by one.

2. Talk with children about why we need potholders and why pot handles and the pot itself are often made of different substances.
3. Place metal and wooden spoons in a hot liquid. See which is a good conductor of heat. What other substances conduct heat?

D. To show that heat expands things
1. Place a balloon over a hot radiator and in the refrigerator. Or place the balloon on the neck of a soda bottle and place the bottle in a pan of hot water.
2. Take a walk to look for sidewalk cracks. Think about why sidewalks do crack and when they crack. Guess why there are tarred lines in sidewalk pavements. Try to figure out ways to open a tight screw-cap jar. In the summer, look at sagging telephone wires. Why do railroad tracks have spaces between them?
3. Place a wire between the backs of two chairs. Place a weight on the wire. Measure the distance of the weight before and after a lighted candle is applied to the wire.

E. To learn about other aspects of heat
1. Demonstrate that heat is reflected and absorbed and that some surfaces and colors retain heat better than others. Place an object like a small rock or a teaspoon under various colors of cloth and under various substances (such as metal, wood, adobe) and expose them to the sun.
2. Talk about summer and hot weather. Ask how people behave on hot days. How do they keep cool in hot weather and warm in cool weather Have a discussion based on the concept that heat is reflected and absorbed.
3. Demonstrate that hot air rises. Sit on the floor and then climb to a high level. Do you feel any difference? Does a thermometer tell you there is a difference?
4. Learn what a thermometer is and how to read it. Take the temperature of basins of increasingly hot water and of ice water. Find the hottest water you can touch and measure how hot it is. Gather a collection of thermometers used for different purposes (candy, meat, weather, oral, etc.) and actually use them. To read a ther-

mometer, a child will have to know how to count by tens and by twos. (It is probably too difficult to teach him this on the spot.) Introduce the symbol for degrees.

F. To find out about sources of heat
   1. Talk about fuels (coal, oil, gas, wood, charcoal), electricity, hot water (steam), the sun, and atomic energy.
   2. Survey the types of stoves and heating systems found in homes. List, using words or drawings, electric appliances that make heat as opposed to those that just give power. Draw pictures of all the electric appliances you can think of. (Use traditional teaching materials on the solar system.) How do you situate a house with respect to the sun? Guess where the big glass windows should be. Look at photographs of an atomic explosion.
   3. Find out how to cook food without a stove. Go on a picnic and cook something over a charcoal or wood fire. Find out ways of cooking that are characteristic of the child's culture. Invite a community member in to demonstrate culturally related cooking techniques.

G. How heat helps us to heat our houses
   1. Begin with noncentral heating such as fireplaces and stoves.
   2. Describe central heating. Furnaces (air heated by contact with hot metal surfaces), and boilers (water heated) send their resulting warm air or hot water throughout the house.
   3. Visit the furnace or boiler room in several buildings. Note the fans used to drive the air and the registers or grills through which it enters the room. In a hot water system, note the larger size of the pipes, the pumps to circulate the water, and the radiators in the individual rooms. Follow the pipes to individual rooms. Private homes are likely to have hot water or forced warm-air systems. Larger buildings use steam heating, requiring more apparatus.
   4. Talk about hot water for our houses. Examine hot-water heaters. Estimate and measure the amount a person uses per day.

5. Discuss how the sources of heat reach the building—delivery of oil, coal, and wood to homes. Include discussion of electricity and gas pipelines owned by utility companies. Visit the basement of a building, try reading meters. Talk about gas deposits and hydroelectric power from dams.

H. Find out how heat destroys bacteria and kills germs.
   1. Food in its natural state remains edible only for a short period of time. Heat (canning) helps to preserve food by destroying the bacteria in it. Canning is one form of food preservation. Some other methods are drying, freezing, refrigeration, smoking, and curing with salt.
   2. Do experiments in which food is left to decay and in which food is canned.
   3. List what types of food are preserved and in what manner. Try to take one food (milk, corn, meat, or a fruit) and see how it can be preserved in several forms. Taste the food in its various forms of preservation.
   4. Talk about milk in its various forms—evaporated and canned, powdered, frozen, and as yogurt and cheese. Make yogurt by adding one cup of commercial yogurt to one quart of milk and placing the mixture in a warm location for twenty-four to forty-eight hours.

I. Vocabulary, colloquialisms, and idioms, associated with heat.
   1. Some examples are—*hot line, hot plate, hot rod, hothouse, hotbed, hot-blooded, hot dogs, hot cross buns, hotheaded, hot foods, hot air, hot* (recently stolen), *hot temper,* animals *in heat, in hot water, hot on the trail, hot from the press, hot on one's heels, the heat of an argument, you're hot,* or *cold* (close to or far from the sought for object or answer).
   2. Repetitious use of these expressions by the teacher in conversation, chants, homemade stories, and recordings.

The Refrigerator

1. Take a walking trip to compare the refrigerator in the school cafeteria (and in the teacher's lounge) with the one in the cooking environment. Look for differences in size, shape, color, and other aspects of appearance.
2. Refrigeration is but one form of food preservation. Find out about other forms such as freezing, dehydrating, and canning. If we do not have a refrigerator, how can food be prevented from spoiling? Find out ways that are characteristic of various cultures—meat preservation by making jerky; cooking the whole animal quickly; and killing large animals only in the wintertime when they can be safely hung outdoors.
3. What does decay look like? Experiment to see what happens to various foods if they are left to decay. Which foods form molds? Which get sour? Which (like eggs) smell offensive? Which foods attract flies? Are there some that don't ever go bad? How would you describe the appearance of decaying meat? What are the various methods by which food grown in one season is stored for use at a later time?

The Sink

1. Find out where the water comes from and where it goes. Trace the pipelines out of the classroom and, if you can, back to the source of the water—the reservoir.
2. Learn about soap. Wash dirty dishes in hot an then cold water, with and without soap. Which combination works best?
3. Look at various forms of soap and detergents—liquid, powder, flakes, soapy steel-wool pads, and cakes of soap.
4. Try making soap. Make soap from the roots of the yucca plant. (Invite a knowledgeable community member to demonstrate). Wash some dirty dishes or shampoo your hair with the yucca soap.
5. Use soap as an art material. Do soap carving. Make soap paintings—mix heavy soap suds and tempera paint and let the children splatter the mixture with their brushes.
6. Blow soap bubbles. Why do they rise? Why do they defy gravity?
7. Talk about the change in volume from detergent in the box to soap suds made from the detergent. How much space does each occupy?

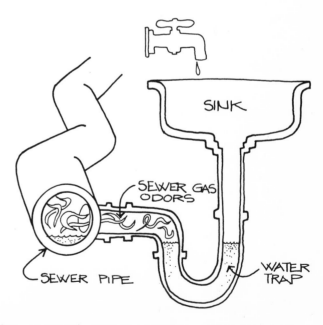

THE WATER TRAP KEEPS SEWER GAS ODORS FROM ENTERING THE SINK BASIN.

When systems are revealed properly, they are almost self-explanatory.

The Cabinets

A. Learning about storage

1. Take a trip to the supermarket to see the various types of containers used for food products—tin cans, glass jars, plastic containers, cardboard boxes, cellophane and plastic wraps, and corrugated or plasticized egg crates. Can you determine which kinds of foods come in which kinds of containers, and why? On the spot, or immediately upon return to school, make pictures of all the different kinds of food storage containers that you see. Make a geometric sculpture from food containers.

2. Talk about storage spaces around the home and in the school. Where do people store dishes, books, newspapers, old rags, pots, food, dresses, socks, toys, wood, or dried corn? Draw pictures of storage utensils.

3. Go on a nature hunt to search for natural containers. You might find tree bark, caves, wells, root cellars, gourds, shells, cones, sand, blocks of ice, and fruit skins.

B. Learning about kitchen tools

1. Cut out pictures from old magazines and newspapers of utensils, small appliances and other objects that belong in a kitchen. Write the word underneath the picture.

2. Learn the names and use of kitchen tools—spatula, wire whisk, tongs, can opener, church key, etc. Guess what each tool might be used for and think of unusual uses for each tool as well.

3. Learn the names and uses of dishes and eating utensils. For example, what is the difference between a plate and a saucer? A plate and a bowl? A glass and a cup?

4. Talk about the electric equivalents of hand-operated tools as, for example, the electric mixer and the whisk; the electric can opener and the manual one. Use both kinds and see if you can determine differences in ease of operation.

Cooking Foods

1. Observe and record changes in volume and texture as food is cooked. Children are unaware and unable to predict that food changes its appearance dramatically when it is cooked. Use this experience to develop observation of changes in volume (mathematics) and to develop language arts vocabulary relative to taste and texture.

2. For example, make soup from a dehydrated mix, from a can, and from scratch. What happens to the textures and volume of vegetables and noodles in each case? What is missing from the packaged dehydrated soups? Take dried foods such as rice, beans, prunes, and apricots and demonstrate how cooking increases their volume. In contrast, what happens to the volume of spinach (or another food with lots of water in it) when it is cooked? Prepare different forms of eggs. Be sure to beat the whites and to add sugar to them for meringues. This is a good activity for studying change in volume.

3. Play sequencing games. Have a set of drawings illustrating the making of a food such as bread. Mix up the cards and have the children sequence them in proper order. Or have them tell you aloud the proper sequence to follow in the recipe *after* they have had the experience of making it.

4. Invite a knowledgeable community member to demonstrate old forms of food gathering, food storage, food preparation, food cooking, food consumption, and food waste disposal—all associated with the culture of the children.

5. Use the cooking environment to introduce children to liquid-measurement terms. In first grade teach them what a pint is and what a quart is, and *have them discover*, by pouring liquids, how many pints make a quart and how many cups there are in a pint. In second grade, you may want to talk about gallons. In kindergarten, you may just want to sequence the pint, half-pint, and quart containers (and pots and measuring spoons as well) by size. Have the children note how much liquids various pots hold and the sizes in inches of various baking tins.

6. Point out various lengths of time. Children have a very poor conception of time. For example, they have little idea of what a half-hour or five minutes really mean and what they can realistically accomplish in those amounts of time; both seem like equally long eternities to them. Cooking (especially using the oven) provides a good opportunity to give children the "feel" of time. Make them aware of what they were able to do in the length of time it took something to cook.

7. Cook some basic inexpensive foods that people of many cultures eat such as corn (tamales, tortillas, grits, cornbread, atole, cornflakes, corn on the cob); beans (frijoles, frijoles refritos, black bean soup, New England baked beans); and greens (lambs-quarters, quelites, dandelion greens, collards, turnip greens, lettuce, spinach).

8. Prepare foods associated with festivals and holidays—posole, Christmas cookies, pumpkin pie, Easter eggs.

9. Cook foods of your region and teach children that these foods are characteristic of your area because they grow well in the soil, etc.

10. Bake bread with and without yeast. Try to determine why yeast makes bread rise. Compare the loaves with and without yeast for size, and compare kneaded and unkneaded loaves for texture.

11. Demonstrate how yeast makes bread rise with the following experiment: Put yeast and sugar together in lukewarm water. Stir the water so that the yeast and sugar dissolve and mix together. Set the mixture aside. In a few minutes the mixture will begin to bubble and foam. Explain that although yeast looks like a powder, it is actually a great many tiny living plants. When the yeast is mixed with sugar in lukewarm water, the yeast plants "eat" the sugar and give off carbon dioxide. This process is called fermentation.

12. Visit stores and industries that do our cooking for us. For example, visit a commercial bread baking firm or a nearby bakery. At a commercial bakery find out what instruments are used to weigh the dough. How is the dough fermented? How long does it take for the dough to rise? How many times must the dough be fermented? Do machines automatically divide the dough into certain sizes? How are air bubbles removed from the dough? Why should air bubbles be removed? How do they make fancy-shaped bread or rolls? How high is the temperature for bread? Compare the cost of a homemade loaf of bread with a store-bought loaf. Ask the children if they think that the homemade loaf is worth the extra cost.

13. Have the children shop for the ingredients they need. Have them keep track of the costs and add up the bill. Have them divide up the total cost of the food by the number of students. (In first grade, this means taking the cost in pennies and dealing the pennies out, like a deck of cards.)

14. Find out what happens to scraps of food that we put into the garbage. (Perhaps you could also study waste disposal and how the garbage collector helps the community.) Have children bring in food scraps such as egg shells or fruit and vegetable peels, and place them in an empty fish tank; add water and a cover, and watch the process of decay for a number of days.

15. Play grocery store. By the time children reach first grade, your classroom grocery store can be more than just a place for dramatic play—it can offer many opportunities for informal practice in arithmetic. Have a pictorial list of prices. Have sale days—two cents off on everything. Have inflation days—three cents more on everything. Have play money, a cash register, empty food containers, adding machine tape, sacks, and a shopping cart, to fully equip your supermarket.

16. Grow your own food. Do more than just planting seeds; try growing them under varying conditions, so that the gardening becomes a science experiment as well. Grow things in the sun and in the shade, with little and lots of water, with and without various kinds of fertilizers. What is the difference in the results? Be sure to write these results down.

Experiences derived from the theme of cooking have been structured for spontaneous, interdisciplinary learning. This model can be generalized to other themes. The point is that the architect can also use this information as design determinants for educational space which truely fosters learning and acts as a three dimensional textbook.

Themes	Principles to be Learned	Suggested Experiences
1. Cultivation	Most corn is grown on farms.	Visit to a cornfield when crop is ready to be harvested.
	Corn is a very tall plant.	Comparing height of children with height of corn as it approaches maturity. Which grows faster?
	The corn kernel is a seed. It is a seed which must be planted anew each year.	Plant seeds in the spring in the school garden or greenhouse.
	Corn is planted in the spring and harvested in the autumn. It takes a certain number of days to reach maturity.	Keep a daily record of the number of days and height to maturity.
2. History	Corn is native to the Americas. *Maize* is another word for corn. It is an Indian word.	Discussion. Reference to ancient artifacts with symbols of corn on them. The word *Maize* is derived from Arawak. (Only North and South American artifacts, languages, history refer to corn.)
	Corn was introduced to Europe and Africa by the explorers. Columbus introduced corn to Europe and Portuguese explorers introduced it to Africa.	(Traditional materials on explorers of the New World.)
	Corn was the survival food of the early settlers.	Discussion. Traditional materials on Pilgrims and First Thanksgiving.
3. Utilization of corn		A display of products made from the corn plant.
a) Food	Corn is a basic food for survival. Corn occurs in many forms. Different Southwestern cultures use corn in different ways. Corn is basic to the diet of all cultures represented in the Southwest. Sometimes different cultures prepare similar foods.	Cooking and eating various foods containing corn: corn on the cob, popcorn, corn oil, corn oil margarine, corn syrup, cornstarch, cornbreads, succotash (from eastern Indians.)
b) Livestock feeds	Animals eat corn. Most corn grown in our country is used to feed livestock. Man in turn eats these animals (hogs, cattle, chickens). Corn husks, stalks, and leaves are winter forage for stock.	Visit to a farm or ranch. Feeding animals.

c) Other uses

Corn is made into many things. Sometimes the use is associated with a particular culture. All parts of the plant can be used.

Using slices from cob in printmaking. Stringing popcorn for Christmas tree. Using the kernels as mosaics. Making wreathes and dolls from the shucks. Using the shucks in tea as a homemade remedy (a black tradition). Making a flute from cob (push out center to cob; make holes along side).

4. Cultural associations

Corn is an integral part of the Indian way of life and religion. It is a symbol of fertility and renewal. In the form of cornmeal, it plays an important role in Indian rituals.

Discussion, films, field trips: 1. Pueblo Indians perform a corn-grinding ceremony in the Spring in which women grind and men sing. There is a corn-grinding song which is available on record. 2. The corn dance is a celebration of the upcoming harvest.

5. Structure of an ear

Classification, matching, and sorting abilities.

With a collection of sweet and Indian corn kernels—sorting, classifying and matching by color, length, and shape.

Have available a collection of seeds of the five principle types of corn. Corn kernels can then be sorted.

6. AN ALTERNATIVE DESIGN PROCESS- FROM CONCEPT TO REALITY

The design and building process described in this book offers an alternative to the traditional architectural process and places environmental modification within the reach of many more people—people who don't necessarily have a design background but who have plenty of energy and a desire for change.

When people want a new building or wish to modify an old one, they usually approach the architect who, after several consultations, begins to design a structure for them. Traditionally, a construction firm is hired, and the plans, once fixed, become the designer's contract to actualize what he has drawn. The plan is fixed or static and the people who will be using the space sit back and wait for the structure to be completed. This process, efficient though it is, may be neglecting the use of valuable design information and energy.

Our process might be thought of as a grass-roots approach, a democratization of architecture. The architect steps down from his classical role and instead opens up design experiences to a group of people. He uses his expertise to expand their awareness so that they can make better aesthetic decisions. He helps these people solve their own problems; he works *with* them, not *for* them. As a result, a reciprocal arrangement evolves. The architect learns more about education, child development, and the real needs of the user, and the user learns more about design.

In this process all participants are actively involved in a project. A trust relationship is possible, and creative thought processes are facilitated. Decision-making of this type gives all participants, including children, a chance to be a *real* part of their environment.

On low-budget projects, volunteer construction is fine. But it must be remembered that paraprofessional help needs much more time than contracted construction. For example, construction on the Monte Vista project was begun and then halted at "safe" intervals to allow the children to use the yet unfinished playground, and to invite them to help in its construction. Our craftsman-carpenter designed the railings; the teachers gave us critiques during construction. As a result, designs changed in the course of the work. In the case of the storage system, money limitations prevented its completion until after children moved into the classroom; once they began using the room, they requested a more flexible and portable system.

The architect steps down from his classical role and opens up the design process to many people—children, teachers, parents.

Aesthetically well-designed classrooms definitely have an effect on learning and the behavior of teachers and children.

The children and parents of the lower grades have plans to help design and build a climbing structure, a water fountain, a suspension bridge, and a sand play area. Some of these items may take several school years to complete, but each will embody the energy and excitement of those who participated. There is no sacred law that says that institutions, especially our schools, cannot change once they are completed.

The point is that people should not get discouraged about the lack of rapid progress on a volunteer project. The time is well spent in such group efforts, provided that the group has a spirit of camaraderie to keep them cohesive. Moreover, it is actually possible to come up with better design solutions after studying how the partially completed space is used.

The teacher's planning area and steps to the weather station.

Many different kinds of wood show children a range of surfaces that are rough, smooth, shiny, light and dark, colored, grained, or planked. Classrooms can be more humane through better design.

Observing Children and the Design Process

In a design process that calls for the creative energies of all the participants, an important role can and should be played by children. The following methods are suggestions for observing and questioning children in various environments. They are ways to collect information about children—their likes, their dislikes, and their behavior both at work and at play.

Classroom Environmental Preference Interview

The Classroom Environmental Preference Interview (CEPI) is designed to determine the children's favorite places in the classroom, through both verbal and nonverbal means. The CEPI is an aid to designers of school environments in discovering the children's environmental preferences. The designers can gain information from the child about his teachers and peers. The CEPI also offers data on the child's ability to communicate verbally and nonverbally.

During individual interviews, each child is asked to draw a picture of his or her favorite place in the classroom. After five minutes, the interviewer asks the child a series of questions to learn where the place is, and how the child would place himself and the other people in the room in his picture.

Children can be experts and they can give us pertinent information about their playground, their school, and what they do after school. All this information should be given to the designer.

Field Procedure

Both the child and the interviewer can sit on the floor with their equipment—a tape recorder, felt-tip markers, crayons, a 14″ by 22″ railroad board, and a stopwatch. The floor-sitting technique puts the interview in a nonauthoritarian posture with the child, and gives the child freedom of movement. The child is asked, "Please draw me a picture of your favorite place in the classroom."

It is recommended that the interviewer take a camera to photograph the room as it exists on that day. The interviewer asks:

1. Where are you in the picture?
2. What do you do there?
3. Where are your friends?
4. Where is your teacher?
5. What do you like to do best in your classroom?

Other data gathered should include the child's birth date, ethnic background, and sex, as well as the teacher's favorite subject and place in the classroom. The interviewer should also note the type of classroom—whether it is open or closed. It is suggested that the economic background of the school neighborhood and population be noted. Code numbers are used to identify the drawings.

PRELIMINARY OBSERVATION SCALE FOR CLASSROOM ENVIRONMENTS

MACRO ENVIRONMENT	+ OBSERVATIONS	SCORING	− OBSERVATIONS
1. Does the exterior of the school appear humanistic as opposed to institutional?		0 1 2 3 4	
2. Is the total school environment utilized as an educational tool?		0 1 2 3 4	
3. Are there resource centers outside the classroom available for use by the children?		0 1 2 3 4	
4. Is access to and from school safe, allowing independent mobility?		0 1 2 3 4	
5. Is there evidence of community playground use?		0 1 2 3 4	

SUBTOTALS: Possible 20; Real _____

CLASSROOM ENVIRONMENT Spaces			
1. Are there specific areas with relevant learning materials?		0 1 2 3 4	
2. Is there a place in the room to get away from other children; a quiet area, a small space for only one or two people?		0 1 2 3 4	
3. Are there any alternatives to the ground plane?		0 1 2 3 4	
4. Is the teacher space (i.e. desk) incorporated with the children's spaces?		0 1 2 3 4	

SUBTOTALS: Possible 16; Real _____

An example of the format for an observation scale to evaluate classrooms.

Child's Poll of Environment

Another way to gain information from children is to set up a polarity scale from which they can make ratings regarding such items as scale, usage of a given area, and multisensory effects.

Observation Scale of Classrooms

The following questions can help you build such an environmental observation scale. The chart on page 136 shows how the data can be collected.

A. Macro environment
1. Does the exterior of the school appear humanistic as opposed to institutional?
2. Is the total school environment utilized as an educational tool?
3. Are there resource centers outside the classroom available for use by the children?
4. Is access to and from school safe, allowing independent mobility?
5. Is there evidence of community playground use?

B. Classroom environment
1. Are there specific areas with relevant learning materials?
2. Is there a place in the room to get away from other children, a quiet area, a small space for only one or two people?
3. Are there any alternatives to the ground plane?
4. Is the teacher space (i.e. desk) incorporated with the children's spaces?
5. Does the child have access to all spaces within the room—unrestricted mobility?

C. Scale
1. Is there general evidence of child-scale?
   a. total room
   b. windows (are they at child height?)
   c. desks or tables
   d. teacher's desk or station
   e. display areas
   f. bookshelves
   g. blackboards
2. Does the overall space complement the child's proportions?

D. Storage
1. Is there a place for each child to put his own personal belongings?
2. Is this storage accessible to the child?
3. Is the storage a visible determinant (open storage)?
4. Are learning materials accessible to the child?
5. Does learning material storage facilitate learning experiences?

E. Organic experiences
1. Are there plants in the room?
2. Are there animals in the room?
3. Are there fish in the room?
4. Is there indoor sand play?
5. Is there indoor water play?

F. Visual equipment
1. Are there bright colors on the walls?
2. Are there graphic patterns on the walls?
3. Are there student-made bulletin boards?
4. Is there evidence that children affect the design of the room?
5. Are there windows in the room?
6. Is there a visible transition between interior and exterior spaces?
7. Is there any creative utilization of the ceiling?
8. Are walls used in a creative manner (e.g. graffiti, wall murals)?
9. Does the floor facilitate activities other than walking or standing (e.g. reaching, drawing)?

G. Traffic flow
1. Is the seating arrangement flexible?
2. Do children enter and leave school areas without having to line up?
3. Are traffic areas free of obstructions?
4. Does the teacher encourage free movement?

H. Playground as learning facilitator
   1. Are there changes of levels in the terrain?
   2. Is a fence used only when necessary (i.e. for a child's safety)?
   3. Is there any creative or sculptured playground equipment?
   4. Is there sand play?
   5. Is there water play?
   6. Is there equipment to challenge a child's psycho-motor development?
   7. Are children unrestricted in use of playground?
   8. Are children allowed to design or alter play facilities?

I. Materials
   1. Are there a number of concrete materials related to a specific concept?
   2. Is there any display of culturally relevant materials?
   3. Are these materials grouped together by some organizational pattern?
   4. Are the materials diversified?
   5. Are materials multisensory in nature?
   6. Are materials graded from sensorimotor toward more abstract?
   7. Are materials related to child-centered experiences?
   8. Are instructional materials generated from the interaction of teacher and child?
   9. Are materials available to children in areas that facilitate child interaction?
   10. Are there teaching machines in evidence?
   11. Are there audiovisual machines available to the children?
   12. Are materials up-to-date?
   13. Are materials designed to function in a variety of different ways?
   14. Have children brought materials into the room?
   15. Are there relevant materials exhibited?
   16. Are there student-made materials?
   17. Is there any evidence of artifacts in the classroom?

Time Lapse Film Documentation

Other observation techniques include a time-lapse film photograph in which a super-8 camera with an automatic time-lapse switch on it is mounted in the ceiling—the shutter clicks every six seconds. By this method a full eight-hour day can be collapsed to approximately three minutes. Time-and-motion studies, traffic patterns, peer-to-peer and peer-to-adult interaction can all be studied at high speed or a frame at a time. A Polaroid camera for the children's use and super-8 movie making are still other ways of collecting information about the school environment.

Conclusion

In the introduction to this book we mentioned that a willingness to change could be an antidote to the traditional classroom blues. By now we hope the appetite has been whetted and energies have been mobilized to begin the task of improving our educational facilities.

Places where our children spend a greater part of their young lives need an imaginative shot in the arm. Better quality learning environments will produce happier children who look forward to school instead of dreading it. Better facilities affect teachers, as well.

But we don't want to give the impression that these renovations and newer teaching methods are easy—they are not. To help children care for a greenhouse every day, to keep weather records, to maintain children's logs, to garden, to do artwork, to do math-science reading, and to listen to a child's woes—all this is truly a taxing proposition. But teachers, housed in our prototype environments, tell us that they and the children are more excited about learning, more open and, despite the extra work, more relaxed. The fervor and enthusiasm felt in this kind of setting may mean the difference between an occupation and a profession and may make a lot of difference to the child whose creative learning potential may have been lying dormant.

The excitement of a dynamic learning situation, where the environment is finely tuned to what the child is all about, and which makes him curious about and responsible for his own learning, is the difference between education for the nineteenth century and preparation for the twenty-first.

BIBLIOGRAPHY

Aaron, D. and Winamer, B. *Child's Play*. New York: Harper & Row, Inc., 1965.

"An Annotated Bibliography on Early Childhood." New York: Educational Facilities Laboratory, 1970.

Ascheim, Skip, editor. *Materials for the Open Classroom*. New York: Dell Publishing Company, 1973.

Borowsky and others. *Yellow Pages of Learning Resources*. New York, 1972.

Boudreau, Eugene H. *Making the Adobe Brick*. Berkeley, California: Fifth Street Press, 1971.

Butler, Annie. *Current Research in Early Childhood Education*. Washington, D.C.: American Association of Elementary Kindergarten-Nursery Educators, 1970.

Caney, Steven. *Toy Book*. New York: Workman Publishing Company, 1972.

Coates, Gary, editor. *Alternative Learning Environments*. Stroudsburg, Dowden Hutchinson and Ross Inc., 1974.

Dattner, Richard. *Design for Play*. New York: Van Nostrand Reinhold, 1969.

Deutsch, C. "Effects of Environmental Deprivation on Basic Psychological Processes." *Art Education Journal of National Art Education Association*, vol. 22, 1:16-18 (January, 1968).

"Diary of a Volunteer Playground." *Landscape Architecture*, April 1973.

"Experience Centered Education," School Zone, Inc., P.O. Box. 603, Corrales, New Mexico.

"Facilities for Early Childhood Education: An Annotated Reference List." Madison, Wisconsin: Educational Resources Information Center.

"Farallones Scrapbook." Farallones Designs, Star Route, Point Reyes Station, California.

"Found Spaces and Equipment for Children's Centers." New York: Educational Facilities Laboratories.

Friedberg, M. Paul and Berkeley, Ellen Perry. *Play and Interplay*. New York: MacMillan Company, 1970.

Frye, D. A. and Standhardt, F. "See More, Hear More, Learn More in Windowless Rooms." *Educational Screen and Audio Visual Guide*, vol. XL (June, 1961).

Hall, E. T. *The Hidden Dimension*. New York: Doubleday, 1966.

Hall, E. T. *The Silent Language*. Garden City, New York: Doubleday, 1959.

Hawkins, Harold. *Appraisal Guide for School Facilities*. Midland, Michigan: Pendell Publishing Company, 1971.

Hennessey, James and Papanek, Victor. *Nomadic Furniture*. New York: Random House, 1973.

Herberholz, Donald and Barbara. *A Child's Pursuit of Art*. Dubuque, Iowa: W. C. Brown, 1967.

Herberholz, Barbara. *Preparing for Early Childhood*. Dubuque: W.C. Brown, 1974.

Hewes. *Let's Build a Playground*. San Francisco: San Francisco Book Co. for Houghton Mifflin, 1975.

Holt, John. *What Do I Do Monday?* New York: Dutton, 1970.

Hurtwood, Lady Allen. *Planning for Play*. Cambridge, Mass.: MIT Press, 1958.

Hurtwood, Lady Allen. *Play and Interplay*. Cambridge, Mass.: MIT Press, 1968.

Kern, Ken. *The Owner-Built Home*. Auberry, Cal.: Homestead Press, 1972.

"Learning—A Magazine for Creative Teaching." 1255 Portland Place, Boulder, Colorado.

Linderman, Earl and Herberholz, Donald. *Developing Artistic and Perceptual Awareness*. Dubuque, Iowa: Brown, 1969.

Linderman, Marlene. *Art in the Elementary School*. Dubuque: W. C. Brown, 1974.

McHenry, Paul, Jr. *Adobe—Build it Yourself*. Tucson: University of Arizona Press, 1972.

Neutra, Richard. "Survival Through Design." *Saturday Review of Literature*, vol. 53, p. 62, (June 6, 1970).

Osmon, Fred. *Patterns for Designing Children's Centers*. New York: Educational Facilities Laboratories, 1971.

Pfluger, Luther W. and Zole, Jesse. "A Room Planned by Young Children." *Young Children*, vol. 24, pp. 6:21 (September, 1969).

Pines, Maya. *Revolution in Learning, the Years from Birth to Six*. New York: Harper & Row, 1965.

"Places and Things for Experimental Schools." New York: Educational Facilities Laboratories.

Proshansky, Harold, Ittelson, W. and Rivlin, L., editors. *Environmental Psychology—Man and His Physical Setting*. New York: Holt Rinehart & Winston, Inc., 1970.

Rolfe, Howard. "Observable Differences in Space Use of Learning Situations in Small and Large Classrooms." Ph.D. dissertation, University of California at Berkeley, 1971.

Rudofsky, Bernard. *Architecture Without Architects*. Garden City: Doubleday, 1964, 1969.

Rudolph, Nancy. *Adventure Playground*. New York: Columbia Teacher's College Press, 1975.

Shapiro, Ben and Boericke, A. *Hand Made Houses: Guide to the Wood Butcher's Art*. California: Scrimshaw, 1973.

Skutch, Margaret. *To Start a School*. Boston, Mass.: Little, Brown & Co., 1972.

Sommer, R. *Personal Space*. Englewood Cliffs: Prentice-Hall, 1969.

Stone, Jeanette. "Play and Playgrounds." National Association for the Education of Young Children, Washington, 1970.

Stone, Mary Anne. *The Cooking Environment*. Unpublished paper, Albuquerque, 1973.

Taylor, Anne P. *A Study on the Effects of Selected Stimuli on the Art Products Concept Formation and Aesthetic Judgmental Ability of Four and Five Year Old Children*, Phoenix, Arizona, 1971.

Taylor, Anne P. "The Effects of Certain Selected Stimuli on the Oral Language Proficiency, Art Products, Concept Formation and Creativity of Four Year Old Non-English Speaking Children," Replication study for the Southwestern Cooperative Educational Laboratory, 1971.

Taylor, Anne P. "Children and Artifacts—A Replacement for Textbook Learning." *Curator*, vol. 16, no. 1 (1973).

Taylor, Anne P. "Prototype Preschool Environment." *Journal of American Institute of Architects*, April 1972.

Taylor, Anne P. "The Effects of Multi-Sensory Cognition Systems on the Concept Formation of Two and Five Year Old Children." *Journal of Research and Development in Education*, Spring, 1973.

Taylor, Anne P. "A Prototype Classroom Environment for Preschool." *Art Teacher*, Winter, 1973.

"The School Primer." Nos. 1-7, Zephyros Education Exchange, 1201 Stanyan Street, San Francisco, Cal.

Winkel, Gary N., editor. *Environment and Behavior*. Beverly Hills: Sage Publications, December 1971. Vol. 3, no. 4.

Woodruff, Asahel. *Concept Formation and Learning. Unit Design in Conceptual Models in Teacher Education*. Edited by John R. Veduin. Washington, D.C.: American Association of Colleges for Teacher Education, 1967.

SOURCES

Activity Resources, P.O. Box, Hayward, California 94545. (An excellent source for math information and manipulatives and interdisciplinary books of projects for children.)

Big Rock Candy Mountain, Portola Institute, Inc., 1115 Merrill Street, Menlo Park, California 94025. (Ideas about materials and media for new education.)

Dick Blick, P.O. 1267, Galesburg, Illinois 61401. (Math and art materials.)

Boston Children's Museum, Boston, Massachusetts. (Matchbox exhibits for classroom use by children; write Benjamin Spock.)

Early Learning Center, 12 Gary Road, Stanford, Conn. 06903. (Summer workshops for teachers to tool up for using a well-designed open classroom.)

Educational Development Center, 55 Chapel Street, Newton, Mass. 02160. (Publications include: "Useful List of Classroom Items that can be Scrounged," "Characteristics of Open Education," "Building with Cardboard," "Building with Tubes.")

Educational Facilities Laboratories, 477 Madison Avenue, New York, New York 10022. (A Ford Foundation sponsored organization to support school planning and to disseminate information regarding school design.)

Group for Environmental Education, 1214 Arch Street, Philadelphia, Penn. 19107.

Museum of New Mexico, Santa Fe, New Mexico. (Kits relevant to Southwestern culture.)

School Zone, Inc., P.O. Box 603, Corrales, New Mexico 87048. (Consultation for school and playground design. Information on how to make the most of the learning environment for teaching purposes. Slide-tape and film on learning environments. Equipment and supply lists for open education. Write for other learning products.)

The Whole Earth Catalogue, Portola Institute, 1115 Merrill Street, Menlo Park, California 94205.

Tri-Wall Containers, Inc., 1 DuPont Street, Plainview, New York 11803. (Source for tri-wall to build cardboard structures.)

Ward's Natural Science Establishment, P.O. Box 1712, Rochester, New York 14603.

Zomes and Solar Energy; Dome Cook Book; Zomeworks—Attention: Steve Baer, P.O. Box 712, Albuquerque, New Mexico 87103.

INDEX